WP

CONTENTS

Published by:
Wilkinson Publishing Pty Ltd
ACN 006 042 173
Level 4, 2 Collins Street Melbourne, Victoria, Australia 3000
Ph: +61 3 9654 5446
www.wilkinsonpublishing.com

In association with:
Zahra Media Group
Publisher of Easy Food and presenter of the Home-Cook Hero Awards
12 Prince of Wales Terrace,
Quinnsborough Road
Bray, County Wicklow, Ireland
Tel: +353 (0) 1 255 7566
Email: info@zahramediagroup.com
Web: www.zahramediagroup.com

International distribution by Wilkinson Publishing with John Blake-Ingram US and associates

National Library of Australia Cataloguing-in-Publication data:
National Library of Australia Cataloguing-in-Publication entry

Creator: Gray, Caroline, author.
Contributor: Doyle, Jocelyn.
Art Director: Kennedy, Nikki.
Title: The best of Irish home cooking cookbook / Caroline Gray.
ISBN: 978-1-925265-76-7 (paperback)
Subjects: Cooking, Irish.
Cooking.
Dewey Number: 641.59415

Photos and illustrations by agreement with Charisse van Kan, Agnieszka Wypych, Pauline Smyth, Jocasta Clarke, Aysecan Tufekcioglu, Erica Ryan, Mikasa Sonnenberg, Sasha Sonnenberg, Leila Saffarian, Sarah de Piña, Joanne Murphy, Dee Daly, Nessa Robbins, Alida Ryder and Bartosz Luczak.

FÁILTE!

Is there anything more comforting than sitting down to a warming beef stew on a blustery winter's night? From the wild Irish seas and rugged coastline to the fertile green fields covering this island, Ireland's stunning landscapes have bred a rich and wonderful food history. It is not one that is overly complex, but rather rooted in the tradition of gathering friends and family around the table to eat, drink and be merry.

I find nothing more nourishing for the soul than being welcomed into my aunt Mary's farmhouse in Castlebar, Co. Mayo with a hug and a cup of tea. We all chat around the stove that warms the room, everyone with a heaping plate of her signature bacon and cabbage. And with so many of us of Irish descent around the world, there is nothing that takes us back to our ancestors' way of life quite like food and the traditions that surround it.

Easy Food magazine has been Ireland's best-selling food magazine for over a decade, so we like to think we know a thing or two about Irish cooking! In these pages, you'll find traditional favourites like Beef and Guinness Stew, Dublin Coddle and Bacon and Cabbage – the dishes that immediately take your taste buds on a trip to Ireland. Of course, no dinner is complete without something sweet to   finish, so pop on the kettle, make your perfect cup of tea and sit down to a slice of Granny's Apple Tart or some Brown Bread with butter and jam. We're even taking you down to the local with pub grub staples like Fish and Chips, Bangers and Mash and even a toasty Irish Coffee to warm you up (and probably impart the legendary 'Gift of the Gab'!).

But you'll also find how Irish cooking has evolved and what Irish home cooks are making today, from the ever-popular Spaghetti Bolognese to Chicken Tikka Masala, and meat-free options like Pearl Barley Risotto. Today's Irish kitchen features recipes from across the world, but it is always the authentic flavours of Ireland at the foundation: creamy butter, hearty grains, rich farmhouse cheeses, tender, grass-fed meat, fresh fish and garden vegetables. Is there anything better?

We've also included a full chapter on award-winning readers' recipes from Irish home-cooks of all ages; some of their recipes have been passed down for generations, while others were last-minute quick-fixes that turned out to be crowd-pleasers! These are the real heroes of home-cooking, and we're delighted to be featuring them here.

Whether you're an experienced cook or a kitchen novice, these tried-and-tested recipes are the perfect way to bring a taste of Ireland home.

Happy cooking!

Caroline

Editor, *Easy Food*

Kitchen basics

COOKING CONVERSION Chart

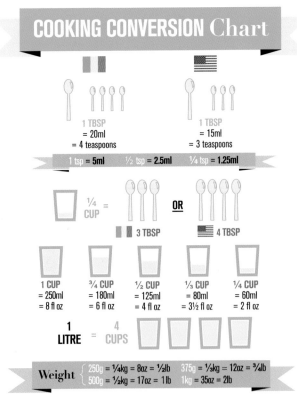

1 TBSP
= 20ml
= 4 teaspoons

1 TBSP
= 15ml
= 3 teaspoons

1 tsp = 5ml   ½ tsp = 2.5ml   ¼ tsp = 1.25ml

¼ CUP =   OR

3 TBSP   4 TBSP

1 CUP	¾ CUP	½ CUP	⅓ CUP	¼ CUP
= 250ml	= 180ml	= 125ml	= 80ml	= 60ml
= 8 fl oz	= 6 fl oz	= 4 fl oz	= 3½ fl oz	= 2 fl oz

1 LITRE = 4 CUPS

Weight {
250g = ¼kg = 8oz = ½lb   375g = ⅓kg = 12oz = ¾lb
500g = ½kg = 17oz = 1lb   1kg = 35oz = 2lb
}

Note: most of the numbers have been rounded off for cookery purposes

OVEN CONVERSIONS

Gas Mark	°C	°F
¼	110°C	225°F
½	130°C	250°F
1	140°C	275°F
2	150°C	300°F
3	170°C	325°F
4	180°C	350°F
5	190°C	375°F
6	200°C	400°F
7	220°C	425°F
8	230°C	450°F
9	240°C	475°F

Temperatures vary so check your oven's instructions. As a basic rule, bear in mind that fan ovens should be set at a slightly lower temperature.

FOODIE QUIRKS YOU'LL ONLY FIND IN IRELAND

1 Crisp sandwiches
It's one of the most sought-after late-night snacks: two slices of soft batch bread, spread with Irish butter and loaded with crunchy crisps. Cheese and onion flavoured crisps are most popular, but salt and vinegar's following shouldn't be ignored! The real question is: do you go for Tayto or King brand crisps?

2 Hot cornflakes
Cornflakes, a bit of milk, into the microwave with a pinch of sugar...pure comfort!

3 Butter on sandwiches
Forget mayonnaise or mustard. The must-have condiment on any sandwich is a good smear of soft butter.

4 Butter on biscuits
Actually, quality Irish butter seems to go well with just about everything! You can't beat a Rich Tea biscuit with a bit of butter and jam.

5 Curry cheese chips
Curry? And chips? With cheese? Yes, it's a delicacy!

6 Red Lemonade
It literally does not exist outside of Ireland, but is a necessary mixer and a staple of Irish summers.

7 Flat 7Up
No other nation would dream of taking all of the fizz out of a fizzy drink, but there's no better cure for an upset stomach!

8 Tea time
Whether you're a Barry's or Lyons household, tea time is sacred! Warm the spotless mugs with a swirl of boiling water, let the tea steep and be sure to have milk and some sugar on hand.

9 Coddle
Explaining to a non-Irish person that you boil sausages and rashers for a stew is worth the funny looks.

10 Breakfast Rolls
There have been several failed missions abroad to find any shop that does a breakfast roll complete with sausages, rashers, pudding, eggs and ketchup.

POTS AND PANS

Don't be lured in by low-cost roasting tins and baking trays; these are often made from thin, low-quality materials that can cause your food to cook unevenly or burn. Follow these tips when investing in tins and trays for your kitchen:

The heavier the better, as long as it can be lifted

- Heavy pans won't warp in the oven and will ensure even heat distribution and baking.
- This will also prevent drippings from burning during long roasts.

Choose the right metal

- Keep in mind that aluminium cookware can react with acidic ingredients, such as lemons or tomato sauce.
- Cast-iron pans are a great investment, but might be too heavy to manage if large joints of meat are added.
- Stainless steel and copper are always good choices, as they are durable and hold up well under most heats.
- Dark-coated tins and trays cook food more evenly and brown better than lighter varieties, as the dark colour allows them to absorb more of the heat.

Avoid non-stick for roasting

- Non-stick cookware is perfect for certain delicate dishes, such as omelettes or pancakes.
- However, they do not allow drippings from roasts to adhere to the pan and develop flavour, which is needed to make homemade gravies and sauces.

A NOTE ON IRISH MEATS

Sausages, rashers and bacon are some of the most commonly used ingredients in many Irish meals, and rightfully so: butchers take great pride in producing top-quality meats here, and small differences show. Read on so you can successfully re-create these recipes at home.

Sausages

- Irish sausages are made from finely-ground pork, seasonings and breadcrumbs. They are softer and more subtly flavoured than American-style breakfast sausage. Look for raw pork sausages or check out online shops for Irish-style sausages.

Rashers

- Irish rashers are traditionally thick-cut bacon slices, more similar to Canadian bacon than American. They contain a bit of the lean back meat and some of the fattier belly meat. Some recipes call for streaky bacon, which is from the belly and the same as American-style bacon.

Bacon

- Recipes like bacon and cabbage require a cured, raw loin of bacon or ham fillet. If you can't find this, just use a smoked ham and skip the boiling stage; a raw pork loin will not have the same salty depth of flavour needed.

VEGETABLE COOKING CHEAT SHEET

Vegetable	Boiled	Steamed	Microwave
Asparagus	Not recommended	8-10 minutes	2-4 minutes
Beetroot	30-60 minutes	40-60 minutes	9-12 minutes
Pak choi	2-3 minutes	3-5 minutes	2-4 minutes
Brussels Sprouts	Bring to the boil and simmer for 5-7 minutes	8-10 minutes	4-6 minutes
Broccoli (Cut Into Florets)	4-6 minutes	5-6 minutes	2-3 minutes
Cabbage (Shredded)	5-10 minutes	5-8 minutes	5-6 minutes
Cauliflower (Cut Into Florets)	4-6 minutes	3-5 minutes	2-3 minutes
Carrots (Sliced)	5-10 minutes	4-5 minutes	4-5 minutes
Aubergine/Eggplant	Not recommended	5-6 minutes	2-4 minutes
Beans	6-8 minutes	5-8 minutes	3-4 minutes
Mushrooms	Not recommended	4-5 minutes	2-3 minutes
Peas	8-12 minutes	4-5 minutes	2-3 minutes
Peppers	Not recommended	2-4 minutes	2-3 minutes
Potatoes (Cut)	15-20 minutes	10-12 minutes	6-8 minutes
Spinach	2-5 minutes	5-6 minutes	1-2 minutes
Courgette/Zucchini	3-5 minutes	4-6 minutes	2-3 minutes

A Hearty START

Easy and wholesome breakfasts

LEMON AND BLUEBERRY PANCAKES

Serves 4

190g/7oz/1½ cups flour
1 tsp salt
2 tbsp sugar, plus extra to serve
250ml/8 fl oz/1 cup milk
1 large egg
3 tbsp butter, melted, plus extra for cooking
Zest of 1 lemon, plus lemon wedges for serving
1 large handful of blueberries

1 In a large bowl, sift together the flour, salt and sugar.
2 Make a well in the centre and add the milk, egg, butter and lemon zest.
3 Stir with a wooden spoon until the batter is smooth and well combined.
4 Heat some butter or oil in a pan over a medium-high heat. Add a ladleful of batter, then lift and tilt the pan so the batter forms a thin, even layer on the bottom of the pan.
5 Cook for three minutes, then flip the pancake and cook for another minute on the other side. Keep warm while you're cooking the rest of the pancakes. Serve with the blueberries, a sprinkling of sugar and a squeeze of fresh lemon juice.

Per Serving 362kcals, 12.1g fat (6.9g saturated), 55.8g carbs, 14.8g sugars, 9.5g protein, 2.7g fibre, 0.702g sodium

THE FRY

Serves 2

Irish butter or olive oil
4 sausages
2 slices of black pudding
2 slices of white pudding
2 ripe tomatoes, halved
2 Portobello mushrooms, stalks removed
1 x 200g/7oz tin of baked beans
4 bacon rashers (back bacon)
4 slices of bread
2 eggs

1 Heat a bit of butter (or oil) in a frying pan over a medium-high heat. Prick the sausages a few times with a fork and add to the pan. Cook, turning occasionally, for about 10 minutes until browned on all sides and cooked through. Transfer to a plate and place in a warm oven.

2 Add the pudding, tomatoes and mushrooms to the pan and cook for 10 minutes until soft. The juices from the black pudding should run clear when pierced. Add to the plate with the sausages in the oven to keep warm.

3 Add the beans to a small saucepan over a medium-low heat. Cook, stirring, for five minutes until warmed through.

4 Cook the rashers in the pan for 3-4 minutes per side until they are cooked through but not too crispy.

5 Pop the bread in the toaster.

6 Heat a bit of butter in the pan and crack the eggs in to fry. Cook for two minutes, then flip and cook for 30 seconds until the whites are set but the yolk is still runny.

7 Divide everything between two plates and serve hot with buttery toast.

Per Serving 591kcals, 29.2g fat (8.8g saturated), 39.8g carbs, 6g sugars, 40.8g protein, 11.5g fibre, 0.71g sodium

MINI GRANOLA BOWLS
Makes about 12

4 tbsp butter, plus extra for greasing
4 tbsp honey
2 tsp cinnamon
¼ tsp salt
4 tbsp apple sauce
1 tsp vanilla extract
300g/11oz/2 cups oats
2 tbsp desiccated coconut (shredded coconut)
4 tbsp ground flax seed
4 tbsp flaked almonds
3 tbsp dried cranberries

To serve:
Vanilla-flavoured Greek yoghurt
Mixed berries
Banana, sliced

1 In a small saucepan, combine the butter, honey, cinnamon and salt.
2 Heat until melted, then remove from the heat and stir in the apple sauce and vanilla.
3 In a separate bowl, mix together the oats, coconut, flax seed, almonds and cranberries.
4 Pour the wet ingredients over the dry and stir until completely coated. Allow to sit for 10 minutes, then place in the fridge for 20 minutes.
5 Preheat the oven to 170˚C/150˚C fan/325˚F/gas mark 3 and lightly grease a muffin tin with butter.
6 Fill each muffin cup about two-thirds of the way with the granola mixture. Using your fingers, press into the centre of each hole and then work your way around the edges to form a small bowl shape. Place in the oven and cook for about 18-20 minutes.
7 Allow to cool completely before removing from the tin. To remove, carefully run a knife around the outside of each granola cup.
8 Store in an airtight container. When ready to eat, fill the cups with yoghurt and top with fresh berries and sliced banana.

Per Serving 189kcals, 8.4g fat (4.9g saturated), 24.9g carbs, 6.6g sugars, 4.2g protein, 3.9g fibre, 0.053g sodium

BEANS, BEANS...
Sweet and smokey baked beans are a favourite option for a quick dinner or tasty snack, and no fry would be complete without them. This homemade version is a great way to control the salt and sugar content compared to the tinned varieties.

HOMEMADE BAKED BEANS
Serves 4

1 tbsp olive oil
1 onion, finely chopped
2 garlic cloves, crushed
400g/14oz tinned cannellini beans
400g/14oz tinned chopped tomatoes
1 tbsp tomato purée (tomato paste)
1 tsp smoked paprika
1 tbsp dark brown sugar
60ml/2 fl oz/¼ cup red wine vinegar
Salt and pepper

To serve:
Toast

1 Heat the oil in a large pan over a medium heat. Add the onion and garlic and stir for 4-5 minutes until the onion is softened.
2 Add all of the other ingredients and season well with salt and pepper.
3 Reduce the heat and simmer, uncovered, for 10-15 minutes until the sauce has reduced slightly. Serve with toast.

Per Serving 412kcals, 4.6g fat (0.7g saturated), 70.4g carbs, 8.8g sugars, 25g protein, 27.1g fibre, 0.035g sodium

RASPBERRY BREAKFAST OATS

Serves 4

1 tbsp butter
150g/5oz/1 cup oats
500ml/17 fl oz/2 cups water
250ml/8 fl oz/1 cup milk
½ tbsp caster sugar
¼ tsp salt
½ tsp vanilla extract
150g/5oz/1¼ cups raspberries, plus extra to serve
4 tbsp walnuts, roughly chopped

1 Melt the butter in a saucepan over a medium heat. Add the oats and cook for 2-3 minutes, stirring until warm.
2 Stir in the water, milk, sugar and salt. Bring to a boil, then immediately reduce the heat and cover with a lid. Simmer for 20 minutes, stirring occasionally, until thickened.
3 Turn off the heat and leave to stand, covered, for about three minutes.
4 Stir in the vanilla extract and raspberries until well combined. Serve with a sprinkling of chopped walnuts and a few extra raspberries.

Per Serving 268kcal energy, 11.4g fat (3.4g saturated fat), 35.0g carbs (5.7g sugars), 9.2g protein, 7.3g fibre, 0.19g sodium

SMOKED SALMON BENEDICT SQUARE
Serves 6

300g/11oz/0.7lb smoked salmon, sliced
6 eggs
Salt and black pepper
2 tbsp fresh dill, chopped

For the pancakes:
2 large eggs
180ml/6 fl oz/¾ cup milk
120ml/4 fl oz/½ cup water
120g/4oz/1 cup flour
3 tbsp melted butter, plus extra for cooking

For the hollandaise sauce:
2 egg yolks
2 tsp water
120g/4oz/½ cup cold butter, cubed
1 tsp lemon juice

1 Whisk together all of the ingredients for the pancakes until smooth. Cover and refrigerate for one hour.

2 Melt some butter in a frying pan over a medium-high heat. Pour some batter into the bottom of the pan, then lift and tilt the pan around so the batter forms a thin, even coating. Cook for 1-2 minutes, then flip and cook for another 30 seconds. Keep warm while you repeat with the rest of the batter.

3 Preheat the oven to 220°C/200°C fan/425°F/gas mark 7. Lay six of the cooked pancakes out on baking trays lined with parchment paper (you may need up to three trays).

4 Arrange some salmon around the centre of each pancake. The salmon should form a square, and also try and leave a square open in the centre for the egg.

5 Carefully crack an egg into the open square in the centre of the salmon. Fold over the edges of the pancake and press down firmly to form a rough square.

6 Bake for about 10 minutes until the egg whites are set and the yolk is slightly runny.

7 Meanwhile, make the sauce. Heat the egg yolks in a bowl set over a saucepan of gently simmering water. Slowly whisk in the water until just combined.

8 Whisk in a cube or two of butter until incorporated, then continue whisking in the butter in batches, only adding another cube once the one before is gone. Stir in the lemon juice and keep warm over a gentle heat.

9 Season the salmon pancakes with salt and pepper. Top with some hollandaise sauce and chopped dill, then serve immediately.

Per Serving 449kcals, 32.7g fat (17.4g saturated), 18g carbs, 2g sugars, 21g protein, 0.7g fibre, 1.261g sodium

€ DF

SOUPS &
Stews

Warm up on a blustery
night with these comforting
favourites

PEA SOUP WITH GARLIC CROUTONS AND FETA

Serves 4

2 tbsp butter
2 leeks, trimmed and chopped
1 small onion, chopped
1l/33 fl oz/4¼ cups vegetable stock
600g/21oz/4 cups peas (fresh or frozen), plus extra for topping
A handful of fresh mint leaves, chopped
2 tsp salt
½ tsp black pepper
80g/3oz/⅓ cup crème fraîche

To serve:
Crispy croutons
2 tbsp Feta, crumbled
A small handful of chives, chopped

1 Heat the butter in a large frying pan over a medium heat and cook the leeks and onion for 10 minutes until soft.
2 Add the stock, increase the heat to high and bring to a boil. Add the peas and cook for five minutes until tender.
3 Remove from the heat and stir in the mint, salt and pepper. Purée the soup with a hand blender, or transfer to a blender to purée in batches.
4 Return to a low heat. Stir through the crème fraîche. Top with croutons, Feta, chives and extra peas to serve.

Per Serving 260kcals, 11.4g fat (6.7g saturated), 31.3g carbs, 10.2g sugars, 10.1g protein, 9.7g fibre, 2.142g sodium

---(◇◇◇)---

WHAT IS CODDLE?
Coddle is a traditional Dublin stew of
inexpensive ingredients slow-cooked
in stock or water. Although there isn't
a specific recipe, it usually includes
pork sausages, rashers, potatoes
and onions.

QUICK DUBLIN CODDLE

Serves 4-6

8 pork sausages
4 bacon rashers (back bacon),
trimmed and halved
8 new potatoes, halved
2 carrots, peeled and sliced thickly
2 red onions, peeled and quartered
Water, to cover
Salt and black pepper
A large handful of fresh parsley,
chopped

1 In a large saucepan, add the sausages,
   rashers, potatoes, carrots and onions.
2 Add enough water to the saucepan to
   cover the ingredients. Season with salt
   and pepper.
3 Cover the pot and place over a high
   heat. Bring to the boil, then reduce
   the heat and simmer for 20-30
   minutes or until the potatoes are
   tender and the sausages are cooked.
4 Stir in the parsley and serve hot.

Per Serving 293kcals, 5.3g fat (1.7g saturated), 50.1g carbs,
5.8g sugars, 11.9g protein, 8.1g fibre, 0.1g sodium

TRADITIONAL IRISH STEW
Serves 4

1kg/35oz/2.2lb lamb neck chops
3-4 bay leaves
4 medium onions, peeled and roughly sliced
800g/28oz/1.7lb carrots, peeled and sliced
1kg/35oz/2.2lb potatoes, peeled and cut into quarters
4 tbsp fresh parsley, chopped
Salt and pepper

1 Put the chops and bay leaves into a large casserole dish and cover with cold water. Bring to a simmer over a medium heat, then cover with a lid and cook on the stovetop (or in the oven at 160°C/140°C fan/325°F/ gas mark 3) for two hours until the lamb is falling off the bones.
2 Remove the bones from the stew and discard.
3 Add the onion, carrots and potatoes. Bring to a simmer and cook for 40-45 minutes until the vegetables are tender, then season to taste. Serve with a sprinkling of chopped parsley.

Per Serving 881kcals, 52.8g fat (25g saturated), 67.4g carbs, 21.1g sugars, 37.9g protein, 6.4g fibre, 0.28g sodium.

SMOKED SALMON BISQUE

Serves 6

60g/2oz/¼ cup butter
1 leek, trimmed and thinly sliced
1 onion, chopped
100g/3.5 oz/2 cups mushrooms, sliced
1 garlic clove, crushed
950ml/32 fl oz/4 cups fish stock
115g/4oz smoked salmon, chopped
400g/14oz tinned chopped tomatoes
2 tbsp fresh parsley leaves, chopped
2 tbsp fresh dill, chopped, plus extra
to serve
Salt and black pepper
3 tbsp flour
250ml/8 fl oz/1 cup milk
300g/11oz/0.7lb salmon fillet, cut into
cubes
250ml/8 fl oz/1 cup cream

To serve:
Crème fraîche

1 Melt the butter in a large saucepan
   over a medium heat and cook the leek,
   onion, mushrooms and garlic for 10
   minutes until soft.
2 Add the stock, smoked salmon,
   tomatoes, parsley and dill. Cook for five
   minutes until heated through. Season
   with salt and pepper.
3 Whisk the flour with the milk and pour
   into the saucepan, stirring to combine.
   Stir in the salmon and simmer for five
   minutes until cooked through.
4 Purée the soup until smooth. Stir
   through the cream and season well.
   Serve hot with a small dollop of crème
   fraîche and some fresh dill.

Per Serving 304kcals, 19.3g fat (8.6g saturated), 11.2g carbs,
4.5g sugar, 21.4g protein, 1g fibre, 0.75g sodium

POTATO AND LEEK SOUP
Serves 4-6

60g/2oz/¼ cup butter
4 potatoes, peeled and diced
3 leeks, sliced
1 onion, peeled and chopped
Salt and black pepper
1l/33 fl oz/4¼ cups vegetable stock
250ml/8 fl oz/1 cup whole milk

To serve:
Chives, chopped
Crispy bacon bits
Cheese and onion soda bread

1 Melt the butter in a saucepan over a
   medium heat. Add the potatoes, leeks
   and onion. Season with salt and black
   pepper and cook for 10 minutes until the
   vegetables are soft.
2 Add the stock, bring to the boil and
   simmer until the vegetables are cooked.
3 Purée the soup until smooth, then season
   to taste.
4 Stir in the milk.
5 Garnish with some chopped chives and
   crispy bacon. Serve with cheese and
   onion soda bread (recipe p.88).

Per Serving 222kcals, 8.8g fat (5.3g saturated), 32.7g carbs, 6g
sugars, 4.7g protein, 4.7g fibre, 0.647g sodium

BEEF AND GUINNESS STEW
Serves 6-8

900g/31oz/2lb lean stewing beef, cubed
3 tbsp oil
2 tbsp flour
Salt and black pepper
Pinch of cayenne pepper
2 large onions, coarsely chopped
1 garlic clove, crushed
2 tbsp tomato purée (tomato paste), dissolved in 4 tbsp water
250g/8oz/½lb carrots, cut into chunks
Pinch of cinnamon
Pinch of ground nutmeg
Sprig of fresh thyme
300ml/11 fl oz/1¼ cups Guinness
3 tbsp fresh parsley, chopped

To serve:
Boiled or mashed potatoes

1 Toss the beef cubes in a bowl with one tablespoon of the oil. In a separate bowl, mix together the flour, salt, black and cayenne peppers. Toss the meat in the flour mixture.
2 Heat the remaining oil in a large casserole dish over a high heat. Brown the meat on all sides (in batches, if required). Add the onions, garlic and tomato purée (tomato paste) mixture. Cover and leave to cook for 5-6 minutes, then remove from the pan and set aside on a plate.
3 Add the carrots, cinnamon, nutmeg and thyme to the casserole dish. Cook for two minutes until the carrots are browned.
4 Pour in some of the Guinness. Bring to the boil and use a wooden spoon to stir up all the bits stuck to the bottom of the dish.
5 Pour in the remaining Guinness. Add the meat and any juices that have collected on the plate. Stir together and season with salt and pepper.
6 Cover the dish and simmer very gently on the stovetop for 2-3 hours until the meat is tender. Remove the thyme, sprinkle with chopped parsley and serve with boiled or mashed potatoes.

Per Serving 272kcals, 11.3g fat (2.8g saturated), 10.1g carbs, 5.7g sugars, 30.7g protein, 1g fibre, 0.7g sodium

Weeknight
COOKING

Quick and convenient, these
dinners keep Irish
families happy

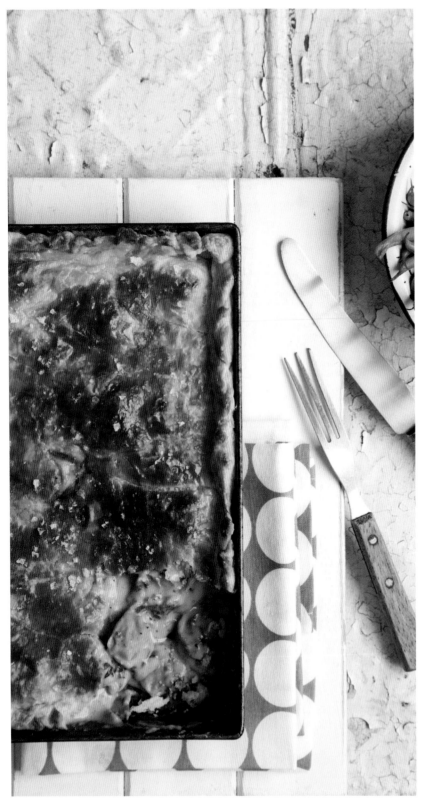

PORK PIE WITH MUSTARD AND MUSHROOMS

Serves 4-6

60g/2oz/¼ cup butter
2 shallots, finely chopped
750g/26oz/1.6lb pork loin, chopped into bite-sized pieces
350g/12oz/6½ cups mushrooms, sliced
2 garlic cloves, crushed
1 tsp dried sage
60ml/2 fl oz/¼ cup brandy
60g/2oz/½ cup flour
500ml/17 fl oz/2 cups chicken stock
200ml/7 fl oz/½ cup cream
2 tbsp wholegrain mustard
Salt and black pepper
1 sheet of frozen puff pastry, thawed
1 egg, beaten with 1 tsp water

1 Melt the butter in a pan over a medium-low heat. Add the shallots and pork and cook for 4-5 minutes, stirring occasionally. Add the mushrooms and garlic.
2 Add the sage and the brandy and cook for 3-4 minutes to cook off the alcohol.
3 Stir in the flour and mix well, then gradually stir in the chicken stock and cream. Bring to the boil and simmer for 20 minutes.
4 Stir in the mustard and cook for another 10 minutes until the meat is tender and the sauce has thickened. Season with salt and pepper.
5 Preheat the oven to 230°C/210°C fan/450°F/gas mark 8.
6 Spoon the filling into a large baking dish. Roll out the puff pastry and place it over the dish, trimming to fit and crimping the edges. Pierce a few slits in the top for the steam to escape.
7 Brush the pastry with the egg wash. Bake for 10 minutes, then reduce the heat to 190°C/170°C fan/375°F/gas mark 5. Bake for another 20 minutes, or until golden brown.

Per Serving 513kcals, 32.4g fat (15.1g saturated), 14.8g carbs, 1.8g sugars, 40.2g protein, 1.2g fibre, 0.63g sodium

CHICKEN KIEV
Serves 4

For the butter:
3 garlic cloves, crushed
Small handful of parsley, finely chopped
90g/3oz/⅓ cup butter, softened
Salt and black pepper

For the Kievs:
4 chicken fillets
100g/3.5oz/¾ cup flour
3 large eggs, beaten
200g/7oz/2 cups breadcrumbs
2 tbsp vegetable oil, for frying

1 Place all the ingredients for the butter into a bowl and season generously with pepper and a little salt. Beat until completely combined. Shape into four logs, wrap in parchment paper and freeze for 30 minutes.
2 Slice a little pocket into the side of each chicken fillet, being very careful not to cut all the way through the meat.
3 Stuff each of the pockets that you made with a butter log. Close the flap by securing each with one or two toothpicks.
4 Place the flour, eggs and breadcrumbs into three separate shallow bowls. Coat each fillet in flour, then egg, then breadcrumbs, then dip back into the egg and finally the breadcrumbs again.
5 Preheat the oven to 200°C/180°C fan/400°F/gas mark 6.
6 Heat the oil in a large pan over a medium-high heat. When hot, cook the chicken Kievs for 2-3 minutes on each side until crispy and golden.
7 Transfer the Kievs to a baking tray and bake for 25 minutes. Serve immediately, making sure to warn people about the toothpicks!

Per Serving 379kcals, 20.1g fat (7.6g saturated), 23.6g carbs, 1.7g sugars, 25.9g protein, 1.3g fibre, 0.26g sodium

CHICKEN TIKKA MASALA
Serves 6

700g/25oz/1.5lb chicken fillets, cut into bite-sized cubes

For the marinade:
250g/8oz/1 cup plain yoghurt
2 tbsp lemon juice
2 tsp ground cumin
½ tsp cayenne pepper
2 tsp black pepper
½ tsp cinnamon
1 tsp turmeric
½ tsp salt
4cm/1.5in piece of ginger, peeled and grated

For the sauce:
2 tbsp butter
4 garlic cloves, crushed
1 green chilli, deseeded and finely chopped
4 tsp ground coriander
2 tsp ground cumin
2 tsp paprika
2 tsp garam masala
2 tsp sugar
1 tsp salt
800g/28oz tinned chopped tomatoes
400ml/14 fl oz/1¾ cups coconut milk
Handful of fresh coriander (cilantro), chopped

To serve:
Steamed rice
Naan bread
Plain natural yoghurt or raita

1 In a bowl, combine all the marinade ingredients. Add the chicken and refrigerate for at least three hours.
2 Melt the butter in a large pan over a medium heat. Add the chicken, discarding the marinade, and cook until brown on all sides.
3 Add the garlic and chilli and cook for one minute. Stir in the ground coriander, cumin, paprika, garam masala, sugar and salt.
4 Stir in the chopped tomatoes and bring to the boil. Reduce the heat and simmer the curry for 15 minutes.
5 Stir in the coconut milk and simmer for another 10-15 minutes.
6 Sprinkle with chopped coriander (cilantro) and serve with steamed rice, naan bread and plain yoghurt or raita.

Per Serving 508kcals, 31.1g fat (19.4g saturated), 21.6g carbs, 7.6g sugars, 38.9g protein, 4.3g fibre, 0.89g sodium

PEARL BARLEY MUSHROOM RISOTTO

Serves 4

2 tbsp olive oil
300g/11oz/4½ cups mushrooms, sliced
2 tbsp butter
2 leeks, chopped
4 garlic coves, crushed
400g/14oz/2 cups pearl barley, rinsed
1 tbsp fresh thyme leaves, chopped
1.2l/40.5 fl oz/5 cups vegetable stock
400ml/14 fl oz/1¾ cups boiling water
60g/2oz/½ cup Parmesan, grated
Salt and black pepper

To serve:
Parmesan shavings

1 Heat the oil in a frying pan over a medium-high heat and cook the mushrooms for five minutes until golden. Use a slotted spoon to transfer them to a plate and set aside.

2 Melt the butter in the pan and cook the leeks for eight minutes until soft and translucent. Stir in the garlic and cook for another minute.

3 Add the barley, thyme, stock and water. Simmer, covered with a lid, for 20-30 minutes until the barley is soft and has absorbed the liquid.

4 Stir in the mushrooms and Parmesan. Season with salt and pepper and serve with shavings of Parmesan.

Per Serving 569kcals, 18.2g fat (7.3g saturated), 88.4g carbs, 4g sugars, 18.1g protein, 17.5g fibre, 0.26g sodium

BETTER THAN BOLOGNESE

Serves 4-6

1kg/35oz/2.2lb stewing beef or
brisket, cut into large chunks
Salt and black pepper
2 tbsp olive oil
1 carrot, chopped
1 onion, chopped
1 celery stick, chopped
3 garlic cloves, crushed
100ml/3 fl oz/½ cup red wine
3 tbsp tomato purée (tomato paste)
800g/28oz tinned chopped
tomatoes
900ml/30 fl oz/4 cups water
1 beef stock cube
2 dried bay leaves

To serve:
450g/16oz/1lb spaghetti
Parmesan, grated
A handful of fresh parsley, chopped

1 Pat the beef dry and sprinkle liberally
  with salt and pepper. Heat one
  tablespoon of the oil in a heavy frying
  pan over a medium-high heat and brown
  the meat on all sides. Remove from the
  pan and set aside.
2 Reduce the heat and add the remaining
  oil. Cook the carrot, onion and celery for
  7-10 minutes until soft but not browned.
3 Add the garlic and cook for one minute.
4 Pour in the wine and bubble until it has
  nearly evaporated.
5 Add the remaining ingredients, including
  the beef and any juices it has released.
6 Increase the heat and bring to a simmer.
  Cover with a lid, reduce the heat and
  cook for two hours until the sauce is
  thick and the beef is tender.
7 Remove the beef and shred it with two
  forks. Stir it back into the sauce.
8 Bring a pot of salted water to the boil
  and cook the spaghetti. Drain, reserving
  180ml/6 fl oz/¾ cup of the water.

9 Add the pasta to the sauce with the reserved water, tossing to coat for 1-2 minutes until
  the sauce thickens.
10 Serve hot with grated Parmesan and chopped parsley.

Per Serving 638kcals, 17.5g fat (5.1g saturated), 52.2g carbs, 6g sugars, 62.9g protein, 2.9g fibre, 0.68g sodium

COMFORTING BACON AND CABBAGE
Serves 6-8

**1.2kg/42oz/2.6lb loin of bacon
(or pork loin, or shoulder of
pork)
750g/26oz/1.7lb Savoy cabbage
60g/2oz/¼ cup butter
Salt and black pepper**

1 Place the bacon in a large pot and cover with cold water. Bring slowly
   to the boil. You may need to change the water several times if the
   meat is salty and produces a white froth on the top of the water – just
   discard and start again with fresh water.
2 Once the boiling water is clear, drain and cover the bacon in hot
   water. Bring to the boil, cover with a lid and leave to simmer for 45-60
   minutes until cooked through. Remove the bacon and keep warm.
   Pour off all but four tablespoons of water from the pot.
3 Meanwhile, remove the tough outer leaves from the cabbage, then cut
   into quarters and remove the central core. Slice the remaining cabbage.
4 Bring the reserved water in the pot to a simmer over a medium-high
   heat. Stir in the butter and shredded cabbage until combined, then
   cover and leave for five minutes. Toss again and season, if required.
   Carve the bacon and serve with the buttery cabbage.

Per Serving 366kcals, 21.4g fat (9.5g saturated), 4.2g carbs, 4.1g sugars, 39.3g protein, 3.3g fibre, 2.2g sodium

STEAK WITH PEPPER SAUCE

Serves 4

**600g/21oz/1.3lb potatoes, peeled and
sliced into thick chips**
2½ tbsp olive oil
4 x 170g/6oz/0.4lb sirloin steaks
Salt and coarse black pepper
3 tbsp red wine vinegar
400ml/14 fl oz/1¾ cups beef stock
120ml/4oz/½ cup cream

1 Place the potatoes in a pot of water
  and bring to the boil. Cook for five
  minutes, then drain and allow to dry.
2 Preheat the oven to 200°C/180°C
  fan/400°F/gas mark 6 and pour two
  tablespoons of the oil onto a baking
  tray. Place the tray in the oven to heat.
3 When the oil is hot, add the potatoes
  and carefully toss. Roast for 30 minutes
  until crispy and cooked through.
4 Heat the remaining oil in a frying pan
  over a medium-high heat and season
  the steaks with salt and lots of black
  pepper. Cook for 2-3 minutes per side.
  Remove the steaks from the heat and
  leave to rest.
5 Pour in the vinegar and bring to a
  simmer. Add the stock and boil for
  7-10 minutes until reduced by half.
6 Stir in the cream and season with more
  black pepper. Serve the steaks with the
  pepper sauce poured over and a side
  of chips.

Per Serving 593kcals, 23.2g fat (10.8g saturated), 24.3g carbs,
2.2g sugars, 47.7g protein, 3.6g fibre, 0.58g sodium

SAUSAGE COMPOTE AND MASH

Serves 4

450g/16oz/1lb pork sausages
2 tomatoes, thickly sliced
1 tbsp olive oil
2 onions, thinly sliced
2 garlic cloves, crushed
100g/3.5oz/½ cup brown sugar
400ml/14 fl oz/1¾ cups cider vinegar

For the mash:
800g/28oz/1.7lb potatoes, peeled
60g/2oz/¼ cup butter
2 tbsp milk

1 Place the sausages and tomato slices on a baking tray lined with foil and grill (broil) for 10-12 minutes until cooked through. Remove from the heat and slice the pork into thick pieces.
2 Heat the olive oil in a saucepan over a medium-low heat. Add the onions, season with salt and pepper and cook for 15 minutes until soft and caramelised.
3 Stir in the garlic and cook for another minute. Add the brown sugar and vinegar and bring to a boil. Reduce the heat and simmer for 20 minutes until the mixture becomes thick.
4 Place the potatoes in a large saucepan of water and bring to a boil. Cook for 20 minutes until tender. Drain and mash with the butter and milk.
5 Stir the pork pieces into the onion compote and gently fold in the roasted tomatoes. Serve over the mash.

Per Serving 590kcals, 31.2g fat (13.3g saturated), 43.5g carbs, 20.9g sugars, 19.5g protein, 4.3g fibre, 0.71 sodium

PORK CHOPS WITH BLACK PUDDING AND APPLE SAUCE

60g/2 oz/¼ cup butter
4 Granny Smith apples, peeled and cut into chunks
50g/2oz/¼ cup sugar
300ml/11 fl oz/1¼ cups cider
600g/21oz/1.3lb pork chops
Salt and black pepper
1 tbsp olive oil
200g/7oz/0.5lb black pudding

To serve:
Roasted vegetables

1 Heat half of the butter in a saucepan over a medium heat and add the apples, sugar and two-thirds of the cider. Bring to a simmer and cook for 10-15 minutes until the apples are soft.
2 Season the pork chops with salt and pepper. Heat the oil in a pan and cook the chops for 3-4 minutes per side until golden brown and cooked through. Remove from the pan, cover with foil and set aside to rest.
3 Add the black pudding to the pan and cook for two minutes per side until crisp. Remove and set aside.
4 Add the remaining cider to the pan and use a wooden spoon to scrape any sticky bits from the bottom. Stir in the rest of the butter.
5 Add the pork chops to serving plates and drizzle over the pan sauce. Top with the crispy black pudding and the apple sauce. Serve with roasted vegetables.

Per Serving 831kcals, 56.4g fat (23.1g saturated), 37.8g carbs, 30g sugars, 41.3g protein, 2.9g fibre, 0.516g sodium

ROAST POTATO BOLOGNESE

Serves 4

1kg/35oz/2.2lb potatoes, peeled
and quartered
1 tbsp olive oil
450g/16oz/1lb beef mince (ground
beef)
4 garlic cloves, crushed
1 tbsp dried oregano
120ml/4 fl oz/½ cup red wine
800g/28oz tinned chopped
tomatoes
2 tbsp tomato purée (tomato paste)
Salt and black pepper
A handful of fresh parsley leaves,
chopped
60ml/2 fl oz/¼ cup cream
90g/3oz/¾ cup Cheddar, grated

1 Place the potatoes in a large pot and fill
with water. Bring it to a boil and cook for
10 minutes until slightly tender.

2 Preheat the oven to 200°C/180°C
fan/400°F/gas mark 6. Add the oil to
a baking tray and place in the oven to
heat. When the oil is hot, carefully toss
the potatoes on the tray and roast for 30
minutes until browned and crispy.

3 Heat the mince (ground beef) in a large
frying pan over a medium heat and cook
for seven minutes until browned, using a
wooden spoon to break up the meat.

4 Stir in the garlic, oregano and wine and
bring to a simmer. Stir in the chopped
tomatoes and tomato purée (tomato
paste). Season well with salt and pepper
and simmer for 15 minutes.

5 Stir in the parsley and cream. Add the
potatoes and stir to combine. Scatter
over the Cheddar and serve hot.

Per Serving 346kcals, 8.9g fat (3.1g saturated), 33.5g carbs,
5.8g sugar, 30.3g protein, 6g fibre, 0.15g sodium

Pub
GRUB

Grab a pint and dig into these
feel-good dishes

TRADITIONAL IRISH COFFEE
Makes 1

30ml/1 fl oz/2 tbsp Irish whiskey
2 tsp soft brown sugar
Strong black coffee
1 tbsp lightly whipped cream
1 tsp cocoa powder

1 Warm a medium-size wine glass or coffee glass with boiling hot water from the kettle. Swirl it around and leave to sit for one minute.
2 Pour out the water and add the whiskey, sugar and coffee. Stir well for 30 seconds to make sure that the sugar is dissolved.
3 Very gently, pour the whipped cream over the back of a spoon onto the coffee, leaving a little space at the top. Spoon some extra whipped cream on top and sieve over the cocoa powder.
4 Don't be tempted to stir! Just sit back and enjoy.

Per Serving 132kcals, 4.9g fat (3g saturated), 7.3g carbs, 5.9g sugars, 1g protein, 0.5g fibre, 0.01g sodium

LOADED POTATO SKINS
Serves 4-6

6 baking potatoes, scrubbed
6 streaky bacon rashers
Olive oil
Salt and black pepper
120g/4oz/1 cup Cheddar, grated
120ml/4 fl oz/½ cup sour cream
3 spring onions (scallions), thinly sliced

1 Preheat the oven to 200°C/180°C fan/400°F/gas mark 6. Bake the potatoes directly on the oven rack for about an hour until cooked through.

2 Cook the rashers in a pan over a medium-low heat for 10-15 minutes until golden and crispy. Drain on a plate lined with kitchen paper (paper towel) and allow to cool, then crumble into small pieces.

3 Remove the potatoes from the oven and allow to cool slightly. Cut in half horizontally. Use a spoon to carefully scoop out the insides, leaving about ½cm of potato in the skins so that they hold together.

4 Turn the oven to 230°C/210°C fan/450°F/gas mark 8. Brush oil all over the potato skins, outside and in, and season with salt and pepper. Place on a rack in a roasting tin. Cook for 20 minutes, flipping halfway through.

5 Sprinkle the insides with grated Cheddar and crumbled bacon. Return to the oven for about 2-3 minutes until the cheese is bubbly.

6 Add a dollop of sour cream to each and scatter with a few chopped spring onions (scallions).

Per Serving 336kcals, 15.2g fat (5.8g saturated), 35.2g carbs, 2.8g sugars, 14.9g protein, 5.4g fibre, 0.572g sodium

BAKED FISH 'N' CHIPS
Serves 4

For the fish:
170g/6oz/7 cups corn flakes
½ tsp black pepper
30g/1oz/¼ cup flour
2 eggs, lightly beaten
450g/16oz/1lb white fish, e.g.
   hake, haddock, cod or halibut,
   sliced into 3cm-wide strips

For the chips:
3 large potatoes, scrubbed and
   cut into chunky chips
½ tsp smoked paprika
Vegetable oil

For the tartare sauce:
2 gherkins (pickles), finely
   chopped
2 tsp Dijon mustard
2 tsp fresh lemon juice
2 tsp Sriracha (optional)
1 tbsp capers
220g/8oz/½ cup plain Greek
   yoghurt
Salt and black pepper

1 Combine all of the tartare sauce ingredients in the bowl of a food processor. Whizz until combined, then refrigerate until ready to use.
2 Preheat the oven to 230°C/210°C fan/450°F/gas mark 8. Bring a pot of salted water to the boil and cook the chips for 6-7 minutes until slightly tender. Drain well, then return to the pan and place back over the stovetop to steam dry for a minute or two, shaking the pan every 20 seconds or so to prevent sticking and to rough up the edges.
3 Transfer the chips to a large baking tray and season with salt, pepper and the smoked paprika. Drizzle with oil, tossing to coat.
4 Bake the chips on the top shelf of the oven for 25-30 minutes until golden brown and crispy, flipping them over halfway through.
5 Meanwhile, in a sealable bag, combine the corn flakes and black pepper. Close the bag and crush the corn flakes. Transfer to a bowl.
6 Place the flour in another bowl and beat the eggs together in a third.
7 One at a time, dip the fish strips into the flour, then the egg, then the crushed corn flakes. Place on a large baking tray.
8 Add the fish to the oven for 10-12 minutes or until cooked through. Serve with the crispy chips and homemade tartare sauce.

Per Serving 583kcals, 8.7g fat (2.7g saturated), 90.3g carbs, 8.8g sugars, 37.7g protein, 10g fibre, 1,263g sodium

€ ❄ ☺ Ⓛ︎Ⓕ︎

TOP TIP
For fried fish, just use the fish batter recipe on p.72.

╭──── ⟨⟨⟨⟨⟩⟩⟩⟩ ────╮

TOP TIP
Sausage rolls are perfect party food.
Just slice them into small bite-sized
pieces before baking for easy serving.

╰──────────────────╯

SAUSAGE ROLLS

Serves 6

250g/8oz/0.5lb pork mince (ground pork)
40g/1oz/¼ cup fresh breadcrumbs
½ tbsp ketchup
½ tbsp mustard
1 tsp Worcestershire sauce
½ tsp soy sauce
½ tsp Tabasco
1 egg, beaten, plus extra for brushing
2 sheets of frozen puff pastry, thawed

1 Preheat the oven to 180°C/160°C fan/350°F/gas mark 4 and line a baking tray with parchment paper.
2 Combine all of the ingredients, except for the puff pastry, in a mixing bowl. Slice each puff pastry sheet in half widthwise, so that you have four equal square pieces.
3 Divide the pork mixture into four portions and form a tube down one end of each pastry sheet.
4 Roll up the pastry, leaving the ends open. Crimp the edges with a fork and brush a bit of beaten egg over the tops.
5 Arrange on the baking tray and bake for 25-30 minutes until golden brown.

Per Serving 710kcals, 41.2g fat (10g saturated), 76.9g carbs, 1.7g sugars, 9.5g protein, 2.5g fibre, 0.36g sodium

SCAMPI WITH CHIPS AND TARTARE SAUCE

Serves 4

For the tartare sauce:
250g/8oz/1 cup mayonnaise
3 tbsp capers, drained and chopped
3 tbsp gherkins (pickles), drained and chopped
1 shallot, finely chopped
Squeeze of lemon juice
3 tbsp fresh parsley, chopped
Salt and black pepper

For the chips:
4 large potatoes, scrubbed
2 tbsp vegetable oil

For the scampi:
450g/16oz/1lb raw prawns (shrimp), peeled (tails left on) and deveined
½ tsp garlic powder
120g/4oz/1 cup flour
1 tsp paprika
2 eggs, beaten
60g/2oz/1 cup panko breadcrumbs
Vegetable oil, for frying

1 Combine all of the tartare sauce ingredients in a small bowl and refrigerate until needed.
2 Preheat the oven to 220°C/200°C fan/425°F/gas mark 7. Cut the potatoes into 1cm-thick chips, leaving the skins on.
3 Bring a pot of salted water to the boil and add the chips. Cook for 4-5 minutes until just barely tender, then drain thoroughly. Return the chips to the pan over the hot stovetop and allow to steam dry for 1-2 minutes, shaking every 20 seconds or so to prevent them from sticking to the bottom of the pan.
4 Transfer the chips onto a large baking tray. Drizzle over the oil and season with salt and black pepper. Toss to coat, then arrange them into a single layer.

5 Bake for 30-40 minutes until crisp.
6 Place the prawns (shrimp) in a bowl and season with salt, pepper and the garlic powder.
7 In a small bowl, stir together the flour and paprika. Place the eggs and panko breadcrumbs into separate bowls.
8 Heat the oil in a deep-fryer or deep-sided pan to 190°C/375°F.
9 Dip each prawn into the flour mixture, then into the egg, and finally into the panko breadcrumbs to coat. Fry in batches for 3-4 minutes or until golden brown, being careful not to over-crowd them.
10 Remove with a slotted spoon and drain on kitchen paper before serving with the chips and tartare sauce.

Per Serving 865kcals, 29.8g fat (5.4g saturated), 108.4g carbs, 29.3g sugars, 40.2g protein, 10.6g fibre, 0.994g sodium

BANGERS AND MASH
Serves 4

For the sausages and onion gravy:
8 pork sausages
2 onions, sliced
½ tsp dried mixed herbs
1 tbsp fresh rosemary, chopped
½ tsp English mustard
600ml/20 fl oz/2½ cups beef stock
Salt and black pepper
2 tsp butter, at room temperature
2 tsp flour

For the mash:
900g/31oz/2lb potatoes, peeled and cubed
60g/2oz/¼ cup butter
120ml/4 fl oz/½ cup milk

1 Preheat the oven to 200°C/180°C fan/400°F/gas mark 6.
2 Place the sausages in a roasting tin. Pierce each with a knife and cook in the oven for 15 minutes, turning once, until browned and crisp.
3 Add the onions to the roasting tin. Mix the dried herbs, rosemary, mustard and stock together in a jug and pour over the sausages and onions. Return to the oven for 20 minutes or until the onions are soft. Season to taste.
4 Meanwhile, cook the potatoes in a pot of salted boiling water for 15-20 minutes until tender. Drain well and then mash.
5 Combine the butter and milk for the mash in a small jug and microwave until melted. Add to the mashed potato and mix until smooth. Season with salt and black pepper, then set aside.
6 To finish the onion gravy, remove the sausages from the tin and mix the softened butter and flour together to form a paste.
7 Place the baking tray onto the stovetop over a medium-high heat. Whisk in the flour and butter mixture for 3-4 minutes or until the gravy has thickened. Add the sausages back to the tray and warm them through for 1-2 minutes.
8 Serve the sausages and mash with the onion gravy spooned over.

Per Serving 404kcals, 20.7g fat (10.6g saturated), 43.6g carbs, 6.1g sugars, 12.4g protein, 7.1g fibre, 0.844g sodium

EASY SHEPHERD'S PIE
Serves 4-6

450g/16oz/1lb potatoes, peeled and cubed
2 tbsp milk
60g/2oz/¼ cup butter
Salt and black pepper
1 tbsp olive oil
450g/16oz/1lb minced lamb (ground lamb)
1 large onion, finely chopped
3 tbsp flour
500ml/17 fl oz/2 cups beef stock
2 carrots, peeled and diced
1 tsp tomato purée (tomato paste)
A handful of fresh parsley, chopped
1 tsp dried thyme

1 Place the potatoes in a large pot and cover with water. Bring to the boil, then reduce the heat and simmer for about 15 minutes until tender. Drain the water, then mash with the milk and half of the butter until smooth. Season with salt and pepper.

2 Meanwhile, heat the oil in a large, non-stick frying pan over a medium-high heat. Add the lamb and cook until browned. Transfer to a plate lined with kitchen paper (paper towel) and keep warm.

3 Heat the remaining butter in a deep frying pan over a medium heat. Add the onion and cook for five minutes until soft.

4 Stir the flour into the onions until coated and cook for one minute.

5 Preheat the oven to 180°C/160°C fan/350°F/gas mark 4.

6 Stir in the stock, carrots, tomato purée (tomato paste), parsley and thyme. Bring to a simmer.

7 Return the meat to the pan and simmer for five minutes to heat through. Pour the mixture into a baking dish.

8 Top with the mashed potato. If the mash has dried out, add a little extra milk to make sure it is creamy enough to spread over the lamb filling. Use a fork to spread the potato across the top.

9 Place in the oven to cook for 30 minutes until golden and bubbling.

Per Serving 311kcals, 15g fat (6.7g saturated), 20g carbs, 3.4g sugars, 23.7g protein, 3g fibre, 0.3g sodium

BEST STEAK SANDWICHES
Serves 4

For the garlic mayonnaise:
2 egg yolks
1 tbsp lemon juice
4 garlic cloves, crushed
120ml/4 fl oz/½ cup olive oil
120ml/4 fl oz/½ cup rapeseed oil (canola oil)
Salt and black pepper

For the steak sandwiches:
450g/16oz/1lb flank skirt steak, at room temperature
1 tbsp butter
50g/2oz/¼ cup brown sugar
2 tbsp olive oil
2 large onions, sliced
120ml/4 fl oz/¼ cup red wine vinegar
4 ciabattas, lightly toasted

To serve:
Rocket (arugula)
Parmesan, shaved

1 For the garlic mayonnaise, pulse the egg yolks, lemon juice and garlic in a food processor until combined.
2 With the blade running, slowly stream in the oils until the mixture is thick. Season with salt and pepper and refrigerate until needed.
3 Place the steak on a chopping board and cover with cling film (plastic wrap). Bash it with a rolling pin to make it all roughly the same thickness.
4 Put the butter, sugar and half of the oil into a large non-stick pan over a medium heat. Once melted, add the onions and cook for five minutes.
5 Add the vinegar and cover with a lid. Turn the heat to low and cook for 25-30 minutes until caramelised. Stir every 10 minutes or so, adding a splash of water if they look dry.
6 Season the steak with salt and black pepper.
7 Place a large, non-stick pan over a high heat until very hot. Rub the steak with the remaining olive oil, then place in the pan. Cook for three minutes on each side for medium, or to your liking.
8 Remove the steak to a plate, cover with tin foil and rest for 4-5 minutes. Slice the steak against the grain into thick slices. Pour the pan juices over the onions and stir to combine.
9 Split open the toasted ciabattas. On the bottom halves, spread on some garlic mayonnaise, then layer over the caramelised onions, steak and some rocket (arugula). Add a few Parmesan shavings and the ciabatta tops.

Per Serving 945kcals, 55.3g fat (29.7g saturated), 69g carbs, 22.4g sugars, 46.6g protein, 3.8g fibre, 0.748g sodium

Kitchen basics

HOW TO CHOP FRESH HERBS

FIRST, rinse your herbs and dry with some kitchen paper (paper towels). Make sure your knife is sharp and the cutting board is clean and completely dry.

CHEF'S KNIFE

Chef's knives are the basic all-purpose knives used for chopping, slicing and mincing. They have broad blades and are typically about 20-30cm (7-11in) in length. They should be rigid, somewhat heavy in your hand and durable. Opt for knives where the blades are forged (a piece of steel is heated and then pounded into shape) rather than stamped (cut out of a sheet of metal).

PARING KNIFE

FOR BASIL, pile the leaves on top of one another and roll into a loose log. Hole the pile at one end and slice into fine ribbons. Do this right before you're ready to use, as cut basil may wilt.

FOR THYME AND ROSEMARY, use your fingers to peel off the leaves from the stems. Gather into a pile and chop finely.

FOR PARSLEY, MINT AND CORIANDER (CILANTRO), gather the whole bunch into your hand and use a knife to slice off the leaves. Roll the leaves into a bunch and chop.

Paring knives are small, rigid knives with pointed tips that are used for small cutting tasks, such as peeling, trimming and paring. Despite its small size, a good paring knife can be quite expensive. They are perfect for any delicate work where a chef's knife would be difficult to use. They are typically only about 5-10cm (2-4in) in length and have quite narrow blades.

SANTOKU KNIFE

Santoku knives are Japanese chef's knives. The blade is about 13-20cm (5-8in) long and curves into an angle at the point. This is an all-around well-balanced knife, as the top of the knife is always in line with the blade, and the blade is the same weight as the handle. Due to the curved edge, they do not have as wide a range of motion as a tradition chef's knife, but are excellent chopping and slicing knives to have in a collection.

FILLETING KNIFE

Filleting knives are about 15cm (6in) in length and are characterised by a narrow, flexible blade. These are ideal for removing raw meat from bones or for filleting fish as they can be maneuvered easily. It is thinner and more flexible than a boning knife, which is also used when working with raw meat.

SERRATED KNIFE

Serrated knives have small ridges along the bottom that make them ideal for slicing breads and baked goods. They have a rounded tip and a rigid blade. Unlike other knives, this is one knife that works just as well when made from stamped, rather than forged, metal. Look for a long blade, one that is at least 20cm (8in) long, as this will make it easier to slice larger cakes and breads.

MASTERING KNIFE SKILLS

Knowing how to properly use your knives sets the foundation for good cooking and helps make efficient work of chopping and slicing your food. Here are a few of the most basic knife techniques; once you start practicing with these, they'll come as second nature in no time!

THE DRAW

Drawing the knife toward you to cut strips of food

Rest the tip of the blade on the chopping board. Place your index finger on the top of the blade; this helps control the knife as you draw it through the food.

Draw the knife toward you, always keeping the blade's tip on the board.

Keep your fingers tucked away from the blade; they will secure the food in place as you continue cutting.

THE SLICE

Pushing the knife away from you to make a basic cut

Rest the knife's handle completely in your palm, keeping a somewhat gentle grip. Keep the tip of the knife on your board in one spot. Lift the knife above the food so it is under the middle portion of the blade as you chop.

Bring the knife down, pushing the blade away from you as it comes down on the board.

Use your spare hand to push the food under the knife as you cut. Curl your fingers away from the blade, making sure your pinky and thumb are safely tucked away.

THE CHOP

Using the entire blade to chop around a pivot point

Hold the knife and place your other hand on top of the blade. Keep the blade's tip on the board and lift the back of the knife.

Rest your hand on top of the blade and bring down the back of the knife, pushing it away from you as you chop. Keep the tip in one spot as a pivot point, chopping in a semi-circular motion.

Use the blade to push and gather the chopped food into a neat pile before going over it again.

THE
Sunday
ROAST

The all-star favourites that
make a Sunday afternoon
so special

CAULIFLOWER CHEESE

Serves 6

1 large cauliflower, trimmed and cut into florets
Salt and black pepper
30g/1oz/2 tbsp butter
25g/1oz/3 tbsp flour
½ tsp English mustard
250ml/8 fl oz/1 cup whole milk
75g/2.5oz/¾ cup medium or strong Cheddar, grated
25g/1oz/¼ cup Gruyère or Parmesan, grated
50g/2oz/½ cup fresh breadcrumbs

1 Blanch the cauliflower florets in a pan of well-salted water for 2-3 minutes until just tender. Drain and rinse under cool running water to stop the cooking process before draining again.
2 Preheat the oven to 200°C/180°C fan/400°F/gas mark 6. Melt the butter in a saucepan and, as it begins to foam, add the flour and mustard. Whisk into a paste and cook over a medium heat, stirring constantly, for about two minutes.
3 Gradually whisk in the milk and continue to stir for about five minutes until the mixture has thickened to a smooth sauce. Add the Cheddar and stir until melted. Remove from the heat, then taste and adjust the seasoning as necessary.
4 Mix together the Gruyère or Parmesan and the breadcrumbs. Arrange the cauliflower florets in a lightly buttered baking dish. Spoon the sauce over the top, then sprinkle over the cheese and breadcrumb mixture.
5 Bake for 20-25 minutes until the top is golden and the mixture is bubbling.

Per Serving 199kcals, 11.8g fat (7.07g saturated), 14g carbs, 4.4g sugars, 9.8g protein, 1.6g fibre, 0.23g sodium

TOP TIP

These potatoes are characterised by their incredibly crispy, flavoursome exterior and fluffy insides.

It's important to heat the fat or oil first in the roasting tin before adding the potatoes; as soon as they hit the hot fat, they'll start crisping immediately. Adding them to warm or room temperature fat or oil won't give you the perfectly crisp texture you're aiming for. Duck or goose fat will have the best flavour, but good olive oil works as well.

THE BEST ROAST SPUDS

Serves 4-6

4 tbsp duck fat or olive oil
700g/25oz/1.5lb floury potatoes, peeled and halved
Salt and black pepper

1 Preheat the oven to 220°C/200°C fan/425°F/gas mark 7.
2 Pour the duck fat or olive oil into a large roasting tin and place in the oven to heat.
3 Meanwhile, place the potatoes in a pot of cold, salted water. Bring to the boil and cook for about seven minutes. Drain well and shake vigorously to rough up their sides.
4 Carefully tip the potatoes into the hot fat. Use a spoon to toss the potatoes until each one is covered. Season with salt and pepper and roast for about one hour, turning halfway, until very crispy and cooked through.

Per Serving 162kcals, 8.6g fat (1.2g saturated), 20.2g carbs, 0.7g sugars, 2.3g protein, 1.8g fibre, 0.007g sodium

SWEET AND STICKY ROSEMARY CHICKEN
Serves 4-6

2kg/70oz/5lb whole chicken
5 tbsp olive oil
2 lemons, 1 juiced and 1 cut into
wedges
1 tbsp honey
200g/7oz/0.5lb shallots, peeled
2 bunches of fresh rosemary
350g/12oz/0.75lb new potatoes
Salt and black pepper

1 Preheat the oven to 190°C/170°C fan/375°F/gas mark 5 and place the chicken in a roasting tin.

2 Whisk four tablespoons of oil, the lemon juice and honey in a bowl. Use your hands to rub half of the mixture under the skin of the chicken onto the meat. Brush the remaining mixture over the skin.

3 Place half of the lemon wedges, half of the shallots and all of the rosemary into the chicken cavity. Arrange the remaining lemon wedges, shallots and the potatoes around the chicken. Drizzle over the remaining oil and season generously with salt and pepper.

4 Roast the chicken for 1½ hours, basting frequently with the pan juices. Increase the temperature to 220°C/200°C fan/425°F/gas mark 7 for 10 more minutes until the chicken is browned and cooked through.

5 Serve everything together on a large platter with the pan juices poured over.

Per Serving 819kcals, 36.8g fat (8.6g saturated), 20.1g carbs, 4g sugars, 98.5g protein, 2.4g fibre, 0.29g sodium

GREAT-WITH-ANYTHING GRAVY

Serves 6

1 onion, roughly chopped
2 carrots, peeled and chopped
2 celery stalks, chopped
Pan drippings from a roast
Juice of 1 lemon
500ml/17 fl oz/2 cups chicken stock
30g/1oz/2 tbsp butter, at room temperature
30g/1oz/4 tbsp plain flour
Salt and black pepper

1 Add the onion, carrots and celery to a food processor and purée until a paste forms.
2 Remove the meat from the roasting tin. Pour the juices from the pan into a jug and allow it to settle. Carefully pour the dark gravy from the bottom of the jug into the tin and discard the clear fat from the top.
3 Set the tin over a medium-high heat and stir in the puréed paste. Cook for a few minutes until combined.
4 Stir in the lemon juice and leave to simmer for one minute.
5 Stir in the chicken stock, scraping up any browned bits from the bottom of the pan, and bring to the boil.
6 Mash the butter and flour in a small bowl, then whisk into the pan until no lumps of flour remain.
7 Reduce the heat and simmer for a few minutes until slightly thickened. Season with salt and pepper, then strain through a sieve to remove any chunky bits before serving.

Per Serving 74kcals, 4.4g fat (2.6g saturated), 7.9g carbs, 2g sugars, 1.2g protein, 1.3g fibre, 0.31g sodium

WHAT IS COLCANNON?
This traditional dish consists of boiled potatoes mashed with wilted cabbage or kale. It is often eaten around Halloween, but it delicious any time of year as a side dish.

COLCANNON WITH BACON

Serves 6-8

1kg/35oz/2.2lb potatoes, peeled and cut into large chunks
8 streaky bacon rashers, chopped
90g/3oz/6 tbsp butter
300g/11oz/3 cups cabbage, shredded
2 spring onions (scallions), chopped
250ml/8 fl oz/1 cup milk
Salt and black pepper

1 Place the potatoes in a large saucepan of cold salted water. Bring to a boil and cook for 15-20 minutes until tender, then drain in a colander and set aside.
2 Return the saucepan to a medium heat and cook the rashers for five minutes until crisp and browned. Remove from the pan and set aside.
3 Melt the butter in the pan and cook the cabbage for five minutes until wilted.
4 Stir in the spring onions (scallions) and continue cooking for one more minute.
5 Stir in the milk to heat through. Add the potatoes and mash, mixing through the greens. Season to taste with salt and pepper and stir in the bacon to serve.

Per Serving 260kcals, 14.1g fat (7.7g saturated), 23.4g carbs, 3.9g sugars, 11.4g protein, 4g fibre, 0.09g sodium

SPRING LAMB WITH YOGHURT, FETA AND MINT SAUCE

Serves 6

1.5kg/53oz/3.3lb leg of lamb
Juice of ½ a lemon
Salt and black pepper
3 garlic cloves, sliced
8-10 small sprigs of fresh rosemary

For the sauce:
250g/8oz/1 cup plain Greek yoghurt
2 tbsp Feta, crumbled
Juice of ½ a lemon
1 tsp extra-virgin olive oil
2 tbsp fresh mint

1 Remove the lamb from the fridge one hour before cooking. Pat it dry with kitchen paper.

2 Preheat the oven to 200°C/180°C fan/400°F/gas mark 6.

3 Rub the lamb all over with lemon juice, salt and black pepper.

4 Make small slits all over the leg of lamb and insert a garlic sliver and a sprig of rosemary into each one.

5 Place the lamb on a rack in a roasting tin, fat side up. Cover the lamb with foil and roast for 30 minutes, then remove the foil and roast for another 40-50 minutes for medium-rare, or until cooked to your liking.

6 Remove the lamb to a board and cover in foil. Allow the meat to rest for 20 minutes before carving.

7 In a food processor, blend the yoghurt, Feta, lemon juice and olive oil until smooth. Season with salt and pepper, then add the fresh mint and pulse to combine.

8 Slice the lamb and serve with the yoghurt sauce.

Per Serving 521kcals, 21.1g fat (8g saturated), 4.1g carbs, 1.8g sugars, 74.6g protein, 1.1g fibre, 0.285g sodium

DIJON-BRAISED BRUSSELS SPROUTS

Serves 6

1 tbsp butter
1 tbsp olive oil
**600g/21oz/1.3lb Brussels sprouts,
trimmed and halved lengthwise**
Salt and black pepper
3 shallots, thinly sliced
120ml/4 fl oz/½ cup white wine
250ml/8 fl oz/1 cup vegetable stock
2 tbsp double cream (heavy cream)
1 tbsp Dijon mustard
2 tbsp parsley leaves, chopped

1 Heat the butter and oil in a saucepan
  over a medium-high heat. Arrange
  the sprouts, cut-side down, in a
  single layer. Season well with salt and
  pepper and cook for five minutes,
  without turning, until golden brown.
  If your sprouts don't all fit in one
  layer, just do this step in batches, then
  return all the browned sprouts to the
  pan when they are done.
2 Add the shallots, wine and vegetable
  stock. Bring to a simmer, then reduce
  the heat and cook, covered, for 15-20
  minutes until the sprouts are tender.
3 Remove the sprouts from the pan
  and set aside. Stir the cream into the
  pan and simmer for 2-3 minutes until
  thickened.
4 Whisk in the mustard and parsley,
  then serve the sauce over the sprouts.

Per Serving 133kcals, 7.3g fat (3.3g saturated), 11.2g carbs,
2.7g sugars, 4g protein, 4.1g fibre, 0.1g sodium

TARRAGON-MUSTARD ROASTED VEGETABLES
Serves 4

800g/28oz/1.8lb new potatoes, halved
450g/16oz/1lb carrots, peeled and roughly chopped
450g/16oz/1lb turnips, peeled and roughly chopped
2 large beetroots (beets), peeled and roughly chopped
1 tbsp olive oil
Sea salt and black pepper
2 tbsp wholegrain mustard
A handful of fresh tarragon, chopped

1 Preheat the oven to 190°C/170°C fan/375°F/gas mark 5. Toss the potatoes, carrots, turnips and beetroot (beets) with oil, salt and pepper.
2 Spread onto a baking tray (or two, if needed) and roast for 35-40 minutes until tender and crisp on the edges.
3 Whisk together the mustard and tarragon. Toss this mixture with the hot vegetables just before serving.

Per Serving 279kcals, 4.6g fat (0.8g saturated), 54.8g carbs, 15.6g sugars, 7g protein, 10.2g fibre, 0.368g sodium

ROAST RIB OF BEEF WITH EASY GRAVY

Serves 6-8

3kg/6.5lb beef rib, on the bone
Sea salt and black pepper
4 tbsp olive oil
2 onions, thickly sliced
1 garlic bulb, cut in half
2 large sprigs of fresh thyme
750ml/25 fl oz/3 cups red wine
500ml/17 fl oz/2 cups beef stock

1 Heat the oven to 220°C/200°C fan/425°F/gas mark 7. Season the meat liberally with sea salt and black pepper, rubbing it into the fat and flesh of the meat.

2 Heat the olive oil in a roasting tin over a high heat and sear the beef for a few minutes on all sides until it is brown all over. Remove the tin from the heat and set the meat aside on a plate.

3 Make a bed of the onions, garlic and thyme in the bottom of the roasting tin and sit the meat on top. Roast in the oven for 20 minutes, then reduce the heat to 170°C/150°C fan/325°F/gas mark 3 and continue to cook until done to your liking. (25 minutes per 450g/1lb for well done, 20 minutes per 450g/1lb for medium or 15 minutes per 450g/1lb for rare.)

4 Remove the meat from the tin, cover with foil and leave to rest for 30 minutes.

5 To make the gravy, place the roasting tin over a medium heat and pour in the red wine. Use a wooden spoon to scrape the crispy bits up from the bottom of the tin.

6 Boil until reduced by half. Add the stock and any juices from the plate. Sieve the gravy to remove the vegetables, pressing down to extract the juices from the onion and garlic. Serve with the beef.

Per Serving 574kcals, 21.3g fat (6.4g saturated), 5.1g carbs, 1.9g sugars, 69.9g protein, 0.6g fibre, 0.362g sodium

ORANGE GLAZED BACON

Serves 6

1kg/35oz/2.2lb loin of bacon
300g/11oz/1 cup orange marmalade
1 tbsp lemon juice
2 tbsp mustard powder
1 bunch of asparsgus, trimmed
300g/11oz/0.7lb carrots, peeled and
sliced into long strips
Salt and black pepper
A handful of fresh parsley leaves, finely
chopped

1 Place the bacon in a large saucepan and
   cover with cold water. Bring to the boil,
   then reduce the heat and simmer for one
   hour until tender, skimming off any white
   froth that collects at the top of the water.
2 Preheat the oven to 180°C/160°C
   fan/350°F/gas mark 4. Whisk together
   the marmalade, lemon juice and mustard
   powder. Place the bacon in a baking dish
   and brush over most of the glaze.
3 Toss the remaining glaze with the
   asparagus and carrots. Season with salt
   and pepper and arrange in the bottom of
   the dish.
4 Bake for 30 minutes, basting the bacon
   occasionally with the glaze. Leave it to
   stand for 10 minutes before slicing.
5 Transfer the asparagus and carrots to a
   serving dish and toss with the parsley.
   Serve warm with the bacon.

Per Serving 311kcals, 8.2g fat (1.3g saturated), 40.3g carbs,
33.1g sugar, 33.7g protein, 2.8g fibre, 0.07g sodium

FROM
The Sea

Bring the rugged Irish seas
home with these fresh recipes

CRISPY COD SANDWICH
Serves 4

350ml/12 fl oz/1½ cups beer
250g/8oz/2 cups flour, plus extra for coating
1 tsp baking powder
1 egg, beaten
Salt and black pepper
450g/16oz/1lb cod fillets, cut into sandwich-sized pieces
3 tbsp vegetable oil

To serve:
Tartare sauce
4 round, soft sandwich rolls, toasted
Coleslaw
Homemade chips
Green salad

1 Mix the beer, flour, baking powder, egg and a pinch of salt in a mixing bowl.
2 Season the cod with salt and pepper and dredge in the extra flour, shaking off any excess. Dip the fish into the beer batter.
3 Heat the oil in a frying pan over a medium-high heat. When hot, cook the fish for 4-5 minutes per side until crispy and cooked through.
4 Spread a layer of tartare sauce on the bottom slice of each sandwich roll. Add a piece of crispy cod, a scoop of coleslaw and the top of the sandwich roll. Serve warm with homemade chips.

Per Serving 773kcals, 22.5g fat (6.8g saturated), 96.5g carbs, 18.3g sugars, 42.3g protein, 3.7g fibre, 0.61g sodium

EASY SEAFOOD CHOWDER

Serves 4

1 tbsp olive oil
1 large onion
1 small leek, chopped
100g/3.5oz/0.25lb streaky rashers, chopped (optional)
1 tbsp flour
500ml/17 fl oz/2 cups fish stock
250g/8oz/0.5lb new potatoes, peeled and cubed
Pinch of cayenne pepper
Salt and black pepper
300ml/11 fl oz/1⅓ cups milk
300g/11oz/0.6lb mixture of fresh fish (e.g. salmon, haddock and cod), cubed
4 tbsp cream
250g/8oz/0.5lb cooked prawns (shrimp)

To serve:
Fresh parsley, chopped
Brown bread (see recipe on p.91)

1 Heat the oil in a large saucepan over a medium heat, then add the onion, leek and bacon, if using. Cook for 8-10 minutes until the vegetables are soft and the bacon is cooked. Stir in the flour and cook for a further two minutes.
2 Pour in the fish stock and bring to a simmer, stirring occasionally.
3 Add the potatoes. Cover and simmer for about 12 minutes until tender.
4 Add the cayenne pepper and some seasoning, then stir in the milk.
5 Tip the fish into the pan and simmer gently for five minutes.
6 Stir in the cream and prawns and simmer for a minute to heat through.
7 Sprinkle with chopped parsley and serve with brown bread.

Per Serving 355kcals, 11.7g fat (2.6g saturated), 22.3g carbs, 6.9g sugars, 40.1g protein, 2.7g fibre, 0.433g sodium

SALMON AND LEEK PIE WITH CHIVE MASH

Serves 4

For the filling:
30g/1oz/2 tbsp butter, plus extra for topping
2 large leeks, sliced
150g/5oz/2¼ cups mushrooms, halved
Salt and black pepper
4 skinless salmon fillets, cut into bite-sized pieces

For the béchamel sauce:
250ml/8 fl oz/1 cup milk
30g/1oz/2 tbsp butter
30g/1oz/¼ cup flour
Pinch of cumin

For the chive mash:
900g/32oz/2lb potatoes, peeled and chopped into chunks
2 tbsp butter, at room temperature
Splash of milk
1 bunch of chives, finely chopped

1 Preheat the oven to 200°C/180°C fan/400°F/gas mark 6.
2 Melt the butter in a frying pan over a medium heat. Add the leeks and mushrooms, season with salt and pepper and cook for 10 minutes until soft. Remove from the pan and add to a large baking dish along with the salmon pieces.
3 Heat the milk in a small saucepan over a medium-low heat until simmering.
4 Melt the butter and flour in the frying pan over a medium heat. Whisk for two minutes to make a smooth paste.
5 Slowly whisk in the milk until completely smooth.
6 Add the cumin and season with salt and pepper. Simmer over a low heat for 15 minutes, stirring regularly.
7 Boil the potatoes in a large pot of salted water until tender. Mash with the butter, then stir in just enough milk until creamy. Season with salt and pepper and stir through the chives.
8 Pour the sauce into the baking dish and stir gently to combine with the salmon and vegetables.
9 Top with the chive mash and use a fork to create small ridges. Dot with a few small knobs of butter and bake for 40-45 minutes until the edges are bubbling and the top is golden.

Per Serving 626kcals, 30.3g fat (13.5g saturated), 48.2g carbs, 7.9g sugars, 43.4g protein, 6.2g fibre,0.258g sodium

POTTED
PRAWNS

Serves 4

2 garlic cloves, crushed
250g/8oz/½lb clarified butter, melted, plus extra for the top
4 tsp fresh thyme leaves, chopped
450g/16oz/1lb cooked prawns (shrimp), peeled
Juice of 2 lemons
Salt and black pepper

To serve:
Crusty bread or crackers

1 Combine the garlic, clarified butter and thyme in a saucepan over a high heat. Bring to the boil, stirring constantly.
2 Add the prawns (shrimp) to the saucepan and cook for 2-3 minutes to warm through.
3 Stir in the lemon juice and season with salt and pepper.
4 Divide the mixture into pots or jars, and cover each with enough clarified butter to form a thin, even layer. Allow to rest until set, or refrigerate until ready to eat. Serve with crusty bread or crackers.

Per Serving 599kcals, 54.3g fat (33.9g saturated), 5.8g carbs, 0.7g sugars, 24.7g protein, 2g fibre, 0.2g sodium

MUSSELS IN IRISH CREAM AND CIDER

Serves 4 as a starter or 2 as a main

900g/32oz/2lb fresh mussels
60g/2oz/¼ cup butter
3 shallots, peeled and sliced
2 garlic cloves, crushed
250ml/8 fl oz/1 cup Irish cider
4 tbsp fresh thyme leaves
**300ml/11 fl oz/1¼ cups double cream
(heavy cream)**
Salt and black pepper
3 tbsp fresh parsley, chopped

To serve:
Crusty bread

1 Wash the mussels in a colander to remove any dirt or grit. Pick through them and remove the stringy "beards" from the edges. Discard any that remain open when tapped on the counter.
2 Place the butter in a large pot over a medium-high heat. Cook the shallots and garlic for one minute, then stir in the cider and thyme.
3 Add the mussels, place the lid on the pot and cook for 3-4 minutes until the mussels start to open. Gently stir the mussels to bring the bottom ones up to the top and place the lid on for another 1-2 minutes.
4 Add the cream, a pinch of salt and pepper and the parsley. Stir to combine.
5 Carefully spoon the mussels into bowls, discarding any that are closed. Pour the sauce and onions left in the pan over the top of the mussels and serve with crusty bread.

Per Serving 370kcals, 18.9g fat (9.6g saturated), 21.7g carbs, 8.5g sugars, 28.1g protein, 1.3g fibre, 0.78g sodium

PEPPERED SALMON IN WHISKEY CREAM SAUCE

Serves 2

1 tbsp black peppercorns, crushed
½ tbsp white peppercorns, crushed
2 x 180g/6oz/0.4lb salmon fillets
1 tsp Dijon mustard
Sea salt
1 tbsp butter
30ml/1 oz/2 tbsp whiskey
120ml/4 fl oz/½ cup double cream (heavy cream)
1 tbsp chives, chopped, plus extra to serve

To serve:
Peas
Mashed potato

1 Combine the crushed peppercorns together in a small bowl.
2 Smear the salmon all over with the mustard, then press the peppercorns into the tops of the fillets to form a thin coating. Season with salt.
3 Place a frying pan over a medium-high heat until hot. Add the butter. Once it starts to foam, lay in the salmon, with the crust facing up.
4 Reduce the heat to medium and cook the salmon for 4-5 minutes.
5 Flip the salmon over and cook for another three minutes. Remove to a plate, cover loosely with foil and rest while you make the sauce.
6 Increase the heat to high and add the whiskey. Boil until reduced by half, then stir in the cream.
7 Use a wooden spoon to scrape up any sticky bits from the bottom of the pan and bring the sauce to a fast bubble.
8 Boil for two minutes until the sauce starts to thicken, then taste and season if necessary.
9 Place the salmon fillets on serving plates. Stir the chives into the pan sauce and pour over the salmon. Garnish with extra chives and serve hot with peas and mashed potatoes.

Per Serving 547kcals, 39.9g fat (19.5g saturated), 4g carbs, 0g sugars, 36.7g protein, 1g fibre, 0.757g sodium

Best
BAKES

Perfect for welcoming friends
and family home – just don't
forget the tea!

STRAWBERRY AND RHUBARB CRUMBLE

Serves 6-8

For the filling:
250g/8oz/2 cups strawberries, hulled and quartered
450g/16oz/1lb rhubarb, chopped
3 tbsp caster sugar (superfine sugar), plus extra if needed

For the crumble:
150g/5oz/1¼ cups plain flour (all-purpose flour)
1 tsp ground cinnamon (optional)
3 tbsp oats
80g/3oz/⅓ cup brown sugar
80g/3oz/⅓ cup cold butter, cubed

1 Preheat the oven to 180°C/160°C fan/350°F/gas mark 4. Combine the strawberries and rhubarb in a mixing bowl and sprinkle with the sugar (you may need slightly more if the rhubarb is very tart). Transfer into a small baking dish.
2 Mix the flour, cinnamon, oats and sugar together in a bowl. Rub in the butter with your fingertips until it is crumbly.
3 Sprinkle the crumble mixture over the fruit and bake for 35-45 minutes until bubbly on the sides and golden on top.

Per Serving 213kcals, 8.2g fat (4.9g saturated), 33.6g carbs, 19.3g sugars, 3g protein, 3.4g fibre, 0.06g sodium

OUR SERVING SUGGESTION
Fancy an afternoon treat? Toast a few slices and slather them with butter and jam.

SODA BREAD
Makes 1 loaf

650g/23oz/5 cups plain flour (all-purpose flour)
1 level tsp salt
1 level tsp bicarbonate of soda (baking soda)
350ml/12 fl oz/1½ cups buttermilk

1 Preheat the oven to 230°C/210°C fan/450°F/gas mark 8.
2 Sieve the flour, salt and bicarbonate of soda (baking soda) into a large mixing bowl. Make a well in the centre and pour almost all of the buttermilk into the well. Mix together with clean hands or a wooden spoon. It will become a soft, spongy dough, but not very wet or sticky. If it is too dry, add a little more buttermilk.
3 Turn the dough out onto a floured work surface and shape it into a disc about 5cm/2in thick.
4 Use a knife to mark the top of the dough with a cross that reaches the sides to "let the fairies out"!
5 Place the bread onto a baking tray and bake for 20 minutes. Reduce the heat to 200°C/180°C/400°F/gas mark 6 and cook for another 25-30 minutes.
6 The bread is done when the bottom of it sounds hollow when tapped. Leave to cool on a wire rack.

Per Serving 251kcals, 1g fat (0g saturated), 51.3g carbs, 1.9g sugars, 7.9g protein, 1.8g fibre, 0.398g sodium

RHUBARB SWISS ROLL
Serves 8

For the cake:
6 large eggs
100g/3.5oz/½ cup caster sugar (superfine sugar)
125g/4oz/1 cup plain flour (all-purpose flour)
2 tsp baking powder
Icing sugar (confectioner's sugar)

For the filling:
200g/7oz/0.5lb rhubarb, chopped
100g/3.5oz/½ cup caster sugar (superfine sugar)
Zest and juice of 1 orange
250ml/8 fl oz/1 cup double cream (heavy cream)

1 Preheat the oven to 190°C/170°C fan/375°F/gas mark 5, then grease and line a Swiss roll tray (23x33cm/9x13in with a 3cm/1in raised edge) with parchment paper. Beat the eggs and caster sugar (superfine sugar) with an electric mixer for about seven minutes until the mixture has doubled in volume. You will know it is ready when you lift the beaters and it holds its shape like a ribbon as it falls back into the bowl.

2 Sift in the flour and baking powder. Fold in gently until just combined.

3 Pour into the lined tray, smooth into an even layer and bake for 20-25 minutes until it comes away from the sides of the tin.

4 When the cake is still warm, turn it out of the tray onto a clean sheet of parchment paper dusted with icing sugar (confectioner's sugar). Roll up carefully from the long end and leave to cool.

5 Combine the rhubarb, caster sugar, orange zest and juice in a small saucepan over a medium-low heat. Heat for 10-15 minutes until the rhubarb is soft but still holds its shape. Leave to cool.

6 Beat the cream until thick, then fold into the cooled rhubarb. Do not fully blend together, but rather aim for a rippled effect.

7 Unroll the cooled Swiss roll and spread with the rhubarb cream mixture. Roll up gently, trying not to squash out the filling. Dust with extra icing sugar to serve.

Per Serving 336kcals, 13.3g fat (7.0g saturated), 49.7g carbs, 35.6g sugars, 7.1g protein, 0.9g fibre, 0.06g sodium

> ### WHAT IS BOXTY?
> Boxty is a traditional Irish potato pancake that contains a mixture of mashed and grated potatoes.

BOXTY LOAF
Makes 1 loaf

1kg/35oz/2.2lb floury potatoes
300ml/11 fl oz/1¼ cups buttermilk, plus a splash
150g/5oz/1¼ cups plain flour (all-purpose flour)
1 tsp salt
Pinch of sugar
¼ tsp bicarbonate of soda (baking soda)

1 Preheat the oven to 200°C/180°C fan/400°F/gas mark 6 and lightly grease a large baking tin with butter.
2 Grate the potatoes into a clean cloth or tea towel, then twist the cloth and squeeze as much liquid out as possible.
3 Place the grated potato in a large mixing bowl and pour in the buttermilk.
4 Add the flour, salt and sugar and stir to combine, forming a thick batter.
5 Mix the bicarbonate of soda (baking soda) with a splash of buttermilk and stir into the potato mixture.
6 Transfer into the prepared tin and smooth to an even layer. Bake for 60 minutes until a skewer inserted into the centre comes out clean.
7 Remove from the oven and let cool on a wire rack. Store wrapped in cling film (plastic wrap) in the fridge for up to five days.
8 When you are ready to serve the boxty, fry thick slices in some butter until golden brown.

Per Serving 136kcals, 0.5g fat (0g saturated), 28.7g carbs, 2.7g sugars, 4.3g protein, 2.8g fibre, 0.304g sodium

WHAT IS A BLAA?
The blaa is a white, floury, very soft
bread roll from County Waterford.

WATERFORD BLAA
Makes 8

1 tbsp active dried yeast
1 tsp caster sugar (superfine sugar)
250ml/8 fl oz/1 cup lukewarm water
500g/17oz/4 cups extra-strong white flour
(bread flour), plus more for dusting
1 tbsp sea salt
1 tbsp butter, at room temperature

1 Dissolve the yeast and sugar in the water and set
  aside for 10 minutes.
2 Sift together the flour and salt in a mixing bowl,
  then rub in the butter. Add the yeast mixture and
  stir until well combined.
3 Turn the dough out onto a floured surface and
  knead for 10-12 minutes until it is smooth, shiny
  and elastic in texture.
4 Place in a clean bowl, cover with a tea towel and
  leave in a warm place for 45 minutes.
5 Turn the dough out onto a floured surface again
  and knock back, pushing the air out of the
  dough. Return to the bowl, cover again with the
  tea towel and rest for 15 minutes.
6 Divide the dough into eight pieces. Roll each
  piece into a ball.
7 Dust a baking dish with flour and add the balls,
  side by side. Sprinkle liberally with flour and leave
  in a warm place for 50 minutes.
8 Preheat the oven to 190°C/170°C fan/375°F/gas
  mark 5.
9 Sprinkle the blaas with a little more flour and
  bake for 13 minutes. Tap on the bottoms of
  the blaas; if they don't sound hollow, give them
  another 2-3 minutes.
10 Place on a wire rack to cool, covering with a
  damp but well wrung-out tea towel to keep
  them soft.

Per Serving 226kcals, 1.8g fat (0.6g saturated), 47.2g carbs, 0.5g
sugars, 7.4g protein, 2g fibre, 0.495g sodium

CHEESE AND ONION SODA BREAD
Makes 1 loaf

**500g/17oz/4 cups plain flour
(all-purpose flour)
2 tsp bicarbonate of soda
(baking soda)
1 tsp paprika
1 tsp sea salt
60g/2oz/¼ cup cold butter,
cubed
125g/4oz/1 cup mature red
Cheddar, grated
1 small onion, grated
2 tbsp chives, snipped
250ml/8 fl oz/1 cup milk
1 tbsp white wine vinegar**

1 Preheat the oven to 220°C/200°C fan/425°F/gas mark 7. Sift the flour, bicarbonate of soda (baking soda), paprika and half of the salt into a mixing bowl. Add the butter and rub it in until crumbly.
2 Stir in the Cheddar, reserving about one tablespoon for the topping. Stir in the grated onion and chives.
3 Whisk together the milk and vinegar, then stir into the mixing bowl.
4 Turn the dough out onto a floured surface and quickly shape it into a round. Transfer to a baking tray and cut a cross into the top using a long knife.
5 Sprinkle the reserved Cheddar and remaining salt over the top. Bake in the centre of the oven for 35-45 minutes, or until it is risen and sounds hollow when tapped underneath.

Per Serving 263kcals, 6.8g fat (4g saturated), 40.5g carbs, 1.7g sugars, 9.2g protein, 1.6g fibre, 0.564g sodium

FLAPJACKS
Makes 16

140g/5oz/⅔ cup butter
6 tbsp honey
170g/6oz/1 cup oats
60g/2oz/½ cup pistachios, chopped
3 tbsp pumpkin seeds
3 tbsp sunflower seeds
60g/2oz/½ cup dried apricots, chopped
60g/2oz/½ cup raisins

1 Preheat the oven to 170°C/150°C fan/325°F/gas mark 3. Butter a 20cm/8in square baking tin and line with parchment paper.
2 Melt the butter and honey in a small saucepan over a low heat.
3 Combine the remaining ingredients in a medium bowl. Pour over the melted butter mixture and stir until everything is combined.
4 Spread into the prepared tin and bake for 35-40 minutes. Remove from the oven and score the bars with a large knife while still warm. When cool, remove from the tray and slice completely.

Per Serving 174kcals, 10.7g fat (1.7g saturated), 18.3g carbs, 9g sugars, 3g protein, 1.8g fibre, 0.08g sodium

BROWN BREAD
Makes 1 loaf

**350g/12oz/3 cups wholemeal flour
(wholewheat flour)
60g/2oz/½ cup plain flour
(all-purpose flour)
1 level tsp bicarbonate of soda
(baking soda)
1 level tsp salt
1 level tsp brown sugar
1 large egg, beaten
1 rounded tbsp black treacle (or
molasses)
400ml/14 fl oz/1¾ cups buttermilk**

1 Preheat the oven to 200°C/180°C
   fan/400°F/gas mark 6. Grease the base
   and sides of a 900g/2lb loaf tin and
   sprinkle with flour.
2 Put all the dry ingredients into a large
   bowl and mix together.
3 In a separate bowl or large jug, mix
   together the egg, treacle (or molasses)
   and buttermilk until combined.
4 Pour into the dry ingredients and mix
   thoroughly with a wooden spoon.
5 Scrape the mixture into the prepared
   loaf tin. Slash the top along the centre
   with a knife so that it will crack evenly
   while cooking.
6 Bake for one hour, or until the bottom
   of the bread sounds hollow when
   tapped and a skewer inserted into the
   centre comes out clean. Cool the bread
   on a wire rack.

Per Serving 160kcals, 1.7g fat (0g saturated), 28.4g carbs, 3.4g
sugars, 7.3g protein, 4.6g fibre, 0.301g sodium

CHOCOLATE BISCUIT FINGERS
Makes 12

400g/14oz/3 cups Digestive biscuits (or graham crackers), crushed
140g/5oz/⅔ cup butter
90g/2oz/½ cup caster sugar (superfine sugar)
1 tbsp cocoa powder
1 egg
200g/4oz/0.25lb milk chocolate, chopped

1 Line a rectangular baking dish with two layers of cling film (plastic wrap) so that there is some hanging over all the sides. Place the biscuit chunks into a large mixing bowl.
2 Melt the butter and sugar in a saucepan over a medium heat.
3 Remove from the heat and stir in the cocoa powder and the egg.
4 Stir this mixture into the crushed biscuits until combined.
5 Pour the mixture into the baking dish and smooth into an even layer.
6 Place the chocolate in a microwave-safe bowl. Microwave on medium power for 30 seconds, then stir. Keep repeating this in 30-second bursts until the chocolate is completely smooth.
7 Spread the chocolate over the biscuit layer. Wrap the cling film over.
8 Refrigerate for at least two hours until completely firm. Lift the mixture out of the dish by pulling up on the cling film, then slice into bars to serve.

Per Serving 363kcals, 22.6g fat (11.2g saturated), 37.2g carbs, 24.1g sugars, 3.8g protein, 1.0g fibre, 0.25g sodium

BASIC SCONES AND VARIATIONS

Makes 6

250g/8oz/2 cups plain flour (all-purpose flour)
1 tsp baking powder
A pinch of salt
90g/3oz/⅓ cup cold butter, cubed
2 eggs
2-3 tbsp milk

1 Preheat the oven to 180°C/160°C fan/350°F/gas mark 4 and dust a baking tray with flour. Sieve the flour, baking powder and salt into a bowl. Prepare the variation ingredients, if they are being used (see below).

2 Rub the butter into the flour mixture until it looks like breadcrumbs. Stir in the variation ingredients, if using.

3 Mix the eggs and milk in a separate bowl. Pour carefully into the dry ingredients, reserving a little of the mixture to glaze the scones later. Mix until combined.

4 Lightly knead the dough on a floured surface. Roll into a disc about 2cm/1in thick and stamp out rounds using a cookie cutter. Place on the baking tray and brush over the reserved egg mixture.

5 Bake for 12-15 minutes until golden brown, then transfer to a wire rack to cool completely.

Per Serving 266kcals, 12.1g fat (7g saturated), 32.6g carbs, 0g sugars, 6.4g protein, 1.1g fibre, 0.12g sodium

Lemon poppy seed scones:
50g/2oz/¼ cup sugar, 3 tbsp poppy seeds and the zest of 1 lemon.

Apple cinnamon and walnut:
50g/2oz/¼ cup sugar, 2 small, diced eating apples, 1 tsp cinnamon and a handful of chopped walnuts.

Banana and honey:
50g/2oz/¼ cup sugar, 2 mashed ripe bananas and 2 tsp honey. No milk is needed if you are using this recipe.

Fruit:
90g/3oz/1 cup berries of choice or raisins.

Cheese and chives:
90g/3oz/1 cup grated Cheddar, 2 tsp chopped chives, ½ tsp mustard powder and ½ tsp chilli powder.

Mediterranean:
2 tsp basil pesto, 6 chopped sun-dried tomatoes and 8 pitted, chopped olives.

APPLE AND CARAMEL UPSIDE-DOWN CAKE
Serves 6-8

2 Granny Smith apples, peeled, cored and thickly sliced
2 tbsp water
1 tbsp lemon juice
300g/11oz/1½ cups caster sugar (superfine sugar)
120g/4oz/½ cup unsalted butter, at room temperature
100g/3.5oz/½ cup brown sugar
4 eggs, separated
90g/3oz/⅓ cup sour cream
1 tsp vanilla extract
160g/6oz/1¼ cups plain flour (all-purpose flour)
1 tsp baking powder
½ tsp ground cinnamon

To serve:
Whipped cream, ice cream or custard

1 Preheat the oven to 180°C/160°C fan/350°F/gas mark 4. Grease a 20cm/8in round cake tin with butter and place on a baking tray lined with parchment paper.

2 Neatly arrange the apples in the bottom of the cake tin. In a small saucepan over a medium-high heat, combine the water, lemon juice, half of the caster sugar (superfine sugar) and half of the butter. Bring to a boil. Cook the mixture without stirring for 8-10 minutes or until it is a rich caramel colour.

3 Carefully and evenly pour the caramel over the apples in the cake tin. Set aside.

4 In a mixing bowl, combine the remaining caster sugar and butter with the brown sugar. Beat until well mixed.

5 Add the egg yolks, sour cream and vanilla. Beat well. Sift over the flour, baking powder and cinnamon, then stir until just combined.

6 In a separate bowl, beat the egg whites with an electric whisk until soft peaks form. Carefully fold the egg whites through the cake batter a little at a time until just combined.

7 Pour the mixture into the cake tin and smooth the surface. Bake for 50 minutes or until a skewer inserted in the centre comes out clean, covering with foil after 30 minutes if the cake starts to look too brown. Allow to cool in the tin for 10 minutes.

8 Run a knife around the edge of the cake tin, then place a serving plate over the top of the tin and invert to release. Serve with cream, ice cream or custard.

Per Serving 448kcals, 16.8g fat (9.7g saturated), 72.4g carbs, 54.7g sugars, 5.5g protein, 1.7g fibre, 0.147g sodium

WHAT IS A TEA BRACK?
Tea brack is a traditional Irish fruitcake
where the dried fruits soak overnight
in cold tea or whiskey, resulting in
plump, flavoursome fruit. It is also
called Barmbrack, which is traditionally
eaten around Halloween.

AFTERNOON TEA BRACK

Makes 1 loaf

250g/8oz/1 cup sultanas
100g/3.5oz/½ cup currants
60g/2oz/½ cup candied peel, chopped
250g/9oz/2¼ cups light brown sugar
300ml/11 fl oz/1¼ cups strong, hot tea
Butter, for greasing
300g/11oz/2½ cups self-raising flour
1 egg, beaten
Pinch of cinnamon
Pinch of ground nutmeg

1 Combine the sultanas, currants, candied
   peel, sugar and tea in a large bowl. Stir
   well, then leave covered for at least eight
   hours for the flavours to combine.
2 Preheat the oven to 150°C/130°C
   fan/300°F/gas mark 2. Grease a 900g/2lb
   loaf tin with butter and line the bottom
   with parchment paper.
3 Stir the flour, egg, cinnamon and nutmeg
   into the fruit mixture. Mix well, then pour
   into the loaf tin.
4 Bake for about 1½-1¾ hours, until well
   risen and firm to touch. Leave in the loaf
   tin for 10 minutes before turning out
   onto a wire rack to cool.

Per Serving 306kcals, 1.1g fat (0.3g saturated), 75.6g carbs,
53.3g sugars, 4.3g protein, 2.5g fibre, 0.13g sodium

GRANNY'S APPLE TART
Makes 1

**225g/8oz/1¾ cups plain flour
(all-purpose flour)
A small pinch of salt
125g/4oz/½ cup cold butter, cubed
150ml/5 fl oz/⅔ cup very cold water
4 large apples, peeled, cored and sliced
3 tbsp caster sugar (superfine sugar), or
more if desired
1 tsp cinnamon (optional)
Milk, for brushing**

To serve:
Custard, whipped cream or ice cream

1 Lightly grease a 23cm/9in round baking tin with butter. Sieve the flour and salt into a large mixing bowl.
2 Rub the butter into the flour until it resembles small crumbs. Stir in the cold water very gradually until the dough just comes together.
3 Divide the pastry in two. Wrap each half in cling film (plastic wrap) and refrigerate for at least one hour.
4 Preheat the oven to 200°C/180°C fan/400°F/gas mark 6.
5 Roll out one half of the pastry on a lightly floured surface so it is slightly larger than the baking dish. Transfer the pastry to the dish, pressing down into the corners and up the sides.
6 Fill the tart with the sliced apples. Sprinkle with sugar and cinnamon, if using. Roll out the other pastry half and use it to cover the filling. Pinch the edges together to seal the tart and form a crust.
7 Brush over the top of the pastry with milk and pierce a small hole in the top for steam to escape. Bake for about 25 minutes and serve warm or at room temperature with custard, cream or ice cream.

Per Serving 364kcals, 17.1g fat (2.8g saturated), 49.6g carbs, 16.7g sugars, 4.1g protein, 4g fibre, 0.198g sodium

Kitchen basics

COOKING TO SCALE

Scaling is a great way to adjust the number of servings a recipe yields. It's a simple process with a few key points to keep in mind:

Cooking temperature: Use the original cooking temperature as a reference point, monitoring closely for the results you are looking for. When cooking more than one dish in the oven at the same time, allow for more cooking time and raise the temperature by about 10-15 degrees.

Cooking time: Stick with the original cooking time as a reference point for how long you should cook the altered recipe. In general, if you are baking half a recipe for cake, bread or pie, then the cooking time will be about two-thirds to three-quarters of the original time.

Dish size: Your best choice is a dish that comes closest to keeping the ingredients to the same depth as the recipe originally called for; so if you are halving or doubling a recipe, use a dish that has half or double the volume of the one called for in the original recipe. You can find the volume by multiplying the dimensions of the original pan.

Other adjustments: If you cannot keep the pan contents to the original depth, then adjust the time, temperature and amount of liquid accordingly:
- When the contents are deeper for dishes that have a lot of liquid, increase the overall cooking time and use a little less liquid, without altering the consistency.

- When they are deeper for baked goods, increase the time and lower the temperature slightly.
- When the contents are shallower for dishes with a lot of liquid, shorten the cooking time and add a little more liquid.
- When they are shallower for baked goods, shorten the time and raise the temperature a bit.

Exceptions: Recipes that do not scale well are delicate foods such as soufflés, baked items requiring yeast, and recipes that prepare a single large item that is meant to be divided into smaller portions, such as some cakes and large joints of meat.

Keep scaling to a minimum: You should avoid scaling a recipe indefinitely. In fact, it's best to increase or decrease a recipe by multiplying or dividing by any number under four. If you must make a lot of a particular dish, it's best to cook it in separate batches following the original recipe.

FLOUR 101

Plain (all-purpose) flour: This flour is made from the endosperm of a wheat grain. It is the most commonly used type of flour and suitable for all types of baking. A raising agent must be added to this for the baked goods to rise.

Self-raising flour: This is plain flour with baking powder added. Many people choose this type as there is no need to add a separate raising agent. It is suitable for all types of scones and muffins.

Wholemeal (wholewheat) flour: This flour contains all of the wheat grain. It has a high fibre content and is used for making brown bread and healthy bakes.

Strong flour: Also called bread flour, this contains a higher percentage of gluten than regular wheat flour and is recommended for baking when using yeast.

Gluten-free flour: This is flour with gluten removed. Therefore it is suitable for those who are coeliac or suffering from gluten intolerance. It can be substituted into recipes instead for regular flour to ensure that the product does not contain gluten, however it may require extra liquid as it is quite dry.

Important tips for baking

- Always preheat your oven.
- Weigh all ingredients very carefully. Use digital weighing scales if possible.
- Use eggs at room temperature, as this helps them combine with the other ingredients.
- Do not open the oven during the recommended baking time.
- When cooling, always place the baked goods on a wire rack to allow air to circulate around them.
- Do not ice or decorate any baked goods until they have cooled completely.
- Don't be afraid to make mistakes or be put off baking if things go wrong. It's the best way to learn!

BREAD-BAKING BLUNDERS... AND HOW TO AVOID THEM

Are you a nervous Nellie when it comes to baking bread? Never fear: these top tips will help you master the art of making everything from traditional Irish soda breads to simple yeast rolls.

- Choose a large bowl so you can mix the ingredients easily. It could be stainless steel or a simple plastic washing-up bowl. It is difficult to mix properly if you feel constricted.

- Baking is an exact science, so measure carefully; otherwise, the results will be inconsistent. Some triumphs, and some dense bricks!
- Mix the dry ingredients thoroughly to ensure that they are evenly distributed before adding any liquid.
- Sieve dry ingredients, especially bicarbonate of soda (baking soda) when needed. Otherwise, little lumps will create dark specks in the bread. Too much results in a yellow-tinged bread that smells and tastes strongly of soda.

- Cool breads on a wire rack so that the air can circulate around the bread; otherwise; the base may turn soggy.
- To keep a soft crust, cover warm bread with a slightly damp, warm, clean tea towel.

Readers'
RECIPES

Award-winning recipes from
Irish home cooks!

CELEBRATING IRISH HOME COOKS

As Ireland's No.1 food magazine, *Easy Food* has always been a champion of home cooking and their annual Home-Cook Hero Awards cooking competition, sponsored by Kenwood, has become a much-loved event in the Irish foodie calendar.

Hand-picked from thousands of recipe entries, 24 finalists from across the country cook for a panel of celebrity judges in a Dublin cookery school, with the aim of ultimately being crowned a Home-Cook Hero. Some of the recipes have been passed down in their families for generations, while others were quick-fix creations that have become hits in their households.

The competition is divided into eight categories, and two special winners were also selected for the top honours of Best Cooking Skills and Easy Food Dish of the Year. Check out all the recipes here, and try them for yourself to bring a bit of authentic Irish cooking into your home!

EASY FOOD DISH OF THE YEAR
Joyce Dougherty
Winter warmer soup with Fermanagh pumpkin bread

BEST COOKING SKILLS
Amy Ryan
Chocolate pizza brownie

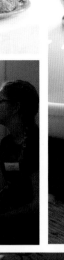

PEA SOUP WITH SMOKED BACON
Serves 3

2 tbsp oil
4 smoked bacon rashers, chopped into small squares
1 onion, finely chopped
1 garlic clove, crushed
400g/14oz/3 cups frozen peas
500ml/17 fl oz/2 cups chicken stock
Salt and black pepper

To serve:
Crème fraîche
Mint leaves
Croutons

1 Heat half of the oil in a pan and cook the rashers until crispy.
2 Remove the rashers and place on some kitchen paper (paper towels) to absorb any excess fat.
3 Heat the rest of the oil in the pan over a medium-high heat and add the onion and garlic. Cook for about three minutes until soft.
4 Add the peas and the chicken stock. Bring to the boil, then reduce the heat and simmer for 8-10 minutes.
5 Add the smoked rashers, but set some aside to garnish.
6 Blend the mixture until it is smooth. Season with salt and pepper to taste.
7 Serve with a spoonful of crème fraîche, a small mint leaf, croutons and the remaining bacon pieces.

Liam Curley
Donadea, Co. Kildare

Winner

 BirdsEye The Food of Life

"I love sports but I seem to get a lot of injuries. I spend a lot of time with bags of frozen peas on parts of my body, so one day when I was sitting with a bag of frozen peas on my head, I decided that it would be a good idea to come up with a tasty idea to use the peas. I think that this soup is so tasty that it is almost worth getting an injury for!"

Per Serving 295kcals, 15.7g fat (3.5g saturated), 23.3g carbs, 8.3g sugars, 16.2g protein, 8.2g fibre, 0.640g sodium

€ ❄ ☺ DF

SIMPLY SAVOURY RICE

Serves 4

1 litre/34 fl oz/4 cups water
375g/12oz/2 cups Basmati rice
150g/5oz/1 cup frozen peas
1 tbsp oil
2 chicken breasts, cut into bite-sized pieces
2 peppers (one yellow and one red), chopped
300g/11oz/4½ cups mushrooms, chopped
1 large onion, chopped
3 tbsp light soy sauce
1 tbsp Chinese 5-spice
1 tbsp Thai 7-spice

1 Bring the water to a boil in a saucepan. Stir in the rice and bring back to a boil, then reduce the heat and cover with a lid. Simmer for 12-15 minutes until cooked and the water is absorbed.

2 Stir the peas into the rice and cover with the lid. Leave for five minutes, then fluff with a fork.

3 Heat the oil in a frying pan over a medium-high heat and cook the chicken for 3-5 minutes, stirring frequently to brown on all sides. Remove from the pan and set aside.

4 Add the peppers, mushrooms and onion to the pan and cook for 5-7 minutes until soft.

5 Stir in the soy sauce and spices. Add the chicken and rice mixture to the pan and heat through.

Per Serving 2417kcals, 4.3g fat (0.6g saturated), 92.5 carbs, 11.6g sugars, 13.3g protein, 4.8g fibre, 3.562g sodium

Sue Butler
Garristown, North Co. Dublin

BirdsEye The Food of Life

"This is a great healthy family recipe. It's lovely eaten as a main course if you add chicken. It's also lovely with sweet chilli sauce, or you can serve it as a side dish with a curry. It's a great dish to prepare in advance because you don't add the rice until the very end. Whenever we have a family gathering this is always on the top of the list. Children love it and they don't even realise they are eating vegetables because they are chopped so small."

TOP TIP
If you can't find potato waffles, just use tater tots or hash brown patties.

POTATO WAFFLES WITH SMOKIN' BAKED BEANS
Serves 4

2 tsp vegetable oil
1 onion, finely chopped
2 garlic cloves, crushed
1 tsp smoked paprika
400g/14oz/1½ cups chopped tomatoes
2 tbsp tomato purée (tomato paste)
2 tbsp caster sugar (superfine sugar)
400g/14oz/1½ cups cannellini beans
Salt and black pepper
8 frozen potato waffles

1 Preheat the oven to 200°C/180°C fan/400°F/gas mark 6.
2 Heat the oil in a pan over a medium heat, then add the onion and cook for three minutes. Add the garlic and paprika and cook for two minutes.
3 Add the chopped tomatoes, tomato purée (tomato paste) and sugar. Stir to dissolve. Stir in the beans and cook for 2-3 minutes to heat through. Season well with salt and pepper.
4 Place the waffles on a tray in the oven and cook for 10 minutes, turning once halfway through.
5 Serve the potato waffles hot with the beans on top.

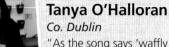

Tanya O'Halloran
Co. Dublin

"As the song says 'waffly versatile', and these certainly are. I always keep some waffles in the freezer along with these tasty, smokin' beans. They are so easy to prepare and in such a small amount of time they make for a perfect meal. What's more is that I live a vegan diet and this tasty snack is perfect for vegans and vegetarians. A winner in my house!"

Per Serving 446kcals, 3.4g fat (0.6g saturated), 74.8g carbs, 13.1g sugars, 25.3g protein, 27.2g fibre, 0.038g sodium

MINTY LAMB BURGER

Serves 4

450g/16oz/1lb lean lamb shoulder mince
(ground lamb)
1 small onion, finely chopped
1 garlic clove, crushed
1 bunch of mint leaves, finely chopped
Salt and black pepper
3 tbsp breadcrumbs
1 egg, lightly beaten
1 tbsp oil

To serve:
Sliced tomato
Fresh Mozzarella, sliced
4 crusty white bread rolls
Iceberg lettuce leaves
Tomato relish

1 Place the lamb, onion, garlic and mint leaves in a large mixing bowl. Season with salt and pepper and mix in the breadcrumbs.
2 Add the egg and bind the mixture together using your hands.
3 Once the mixture is well combined, cover with cling film (plastic wrap) and refrigerate for 20 minutes.
4 Remove the mixture from the fridge and shape into four evenly-sized burgers.
5 Heat the oil in a pan over a medium heat and cook the burgers for five minutes on each side or until cooked through.
6 Remove the pan from the heat and cover with a lid or some tin foil. Leave the burgers to rest for five minutes.
7 While the burgers are resting, garnish the plate with some of the tomato slices and the Mozzarella. Warm the rolls in the oven.
8 Serve the burgers on the rolls with the lettuce, tomato relish and sliced tomatoes.

Per Serving 611kcals, 23g fat (4.4g saturated), 66g carbs, 6.7g sugars, 36.9g protein, 22.3g fibre, 0.348g sodium

Rory Donegan
Midleton, Co. Cork   *Winner*   Mr·CRUMB
"This recipe means a lot to me; my Mam doesn't eat lamb and my Dad doesn't usually eat burgers, but he really likes lamb, so I decided to get them to try it and they ended up loving it. My sister would never eat mint-flavoured food so I did not tell her about the mint and she absolutely loves it now. I chose lamb because it was a meat I didn't really know, but I started experimenting with it and now it is my favourite. Lamb burgers are the big one in the Donegan household now."

50g poppy seeds
3 tbsp parsley, finely chopped

For the dressing:
60ml/2oz/¼ cup cider vinegar
200g/7oz/¾ cup mayonnaise
5 tbsp honey
1 tsp salt
1 tsp pepper

To serve:
Hamburger buns
Tomato and chilli chutney
Mayonnaise
Lettuce
Tomatoes
Onion

For the fries:
3 potatoes, peeled and cut into chunky chips

1 Mix together all of the ingredients for the burgers, except for the oil, in a bowl. Shape into six burgers, then refrigerate for 15 minutes.
2 Meanwhile, add the potatoes to a pot and cover with water. Bring to a boil and cook for four minutes. Drain and pat them dry with kitchen paper (paper towels).
3 Heat some oil in a frying pan over a medium-high heat. Cook the chips for five minutes, turning halfway through, until crispy and golden.
4 Wipe the pan clean and heat a drizzle of oil. Cook the burgers, in batches if necessary, for 3-5 minutes on each side. Remove from the heat and set aside to rest.
5 Combine all the ingredients for the coleslaw in a bowl.
6 Mix the ingredients for the dressing in a small bowl and pour over the coleslaw. Combine right before serving.
7 Serve the burgers in the rolls with chutney, mayonnaise, lettuce, tomatoes and onion.

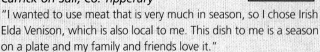

Elizabeth Butler
Carrick-on-Suir, Co. Tipperary
"I wanted to use meat that is very much in season, so I chose Irish Elda Venison, which is also local to me. This dish to me is a season on a plate and my family and friends love it."

SWEET AND SPICY VENISON BURGER
Serves 6

For the burger mix:
450g/16oz/1lb venison mince (ground venison)
150g/5oz/0.3lb pork mince (ground pork)
120g/4oz/1 cup breadcrumbs
1 tsp cayenne pepper
1 tsp smoked paprika
1 tsp onion powder
3 tbsp fresh parsley, finely chopped
1 egg yolk
Salt and black pepper
Vegetable oil, for cooking

For the apple coleslaw:
½ head of white cabbage, finely shredded
2 carrots, grated
2 Granny Smith apples, grated
2 spring onions (scallions), finely sliced

Per Serving 489kcals, 19.2g fat (2.6g saturated), 58.4g carbs, 27.3g sugars, 22.8g protein, 5.4g fibre, 0.658g sodium

PEPPERONI PIZZA BURGER

Serves 4

60g/2oz/1 cup chorizo (Spanish-style smoked sausage), finely chopped
650g/23oz/1.5lb beef mince (ground beef)
60g/2oz/½ cup breadcrumbs
1 egg
3 tbsp fresh basil, finely chopped
2 garlic cloves, crushed
Salt and black pepper
1 tbsp oil
8 slices Mozzarella
8 slices pepperoni
30g/1oz/2 tbsp butter, at room temperature
4 burger buns
8 tbsp marinara sauce

To serve:
Rocket leaves (arugula)
Cherry tomatoes, sliced

1 Combine the chorizo, beef, breadcrumbs, egg, basil, half of the garlic and a pinch of salt and pepper in a mixing bowl. Form the mixture into four burger patties.
2 Heat the oil in a frying pan over a medium-high heat and cook the burgers for 3-4 minutes on each side.
3 When cooked, top each burger with two slices of Mozzarella and two slices of pepperoni.
4 Mix the rest of the garlic with the butter and spread onto the buns. Toast the buns on a dry skillet until golden, then spread the marinara sauce onto them.
5 Add the patties to the buns and top each with rocket and cherry tomatoes.

Per Serving 764kcals, 43.3g fat (19.4g saturated), 16.4g carbs, 2.9g sugars,74.2g protein, 1.1g fibre, 0.985g sodium

Kellyann McGann
Dungourney, Co. Cork

"I fell in love with this pizza burger after tasting one similar on holidays. My pizza burger combines a popular Italian dish with a popular American dish. This burger has many different flavours and aromas from the delicious tomato sauce to the spicy pepperoni and chorizo, which is guaranteed to make your mouth water. It's a very simple recipe to follow for all ages. I put my own twist to this and it's a family favourite in my house."

JILL'S FAMOUS MAC AND CHEESE
Serves 4

450g/16oz/1lb macaroni
2 tbsp olive oil
4 tbsp butter
100g/3.5oz/1 cup breadcrumbs
Salt and black pepper
3 tbsp plain flour (all-purpose flour)
500ml/17 fl oz/2 cups milk
¼ tsp nutmeg
¼ tsp mustard powder
100g/3.5oz/1 cup mature Cheddar, grated
50g/2oz/½ cup Parmesan, plus extra for topping
250ml/8 fl oz/1 cup cream

To serve:
Garlic bread

1 Preheat the oven to 200°C/180°C fan/400°F/gas mark 6. Bring a pot of salted water to the boil. Add the macaroni and half of the oil. Cook for 9-11 minutes until al dente.
2 Drain the pasta and rinse in cool water. Toss in the rest of the olive oil to prevent clumping, then set aside.
3 Melt one tablespoon of butter in a frying pan. Stir in the breadcrumbs and some salt, then remove from the heat.
4 In a medium saucepan, melt the rest of the butter and add the flour gradually, constantly whisking until a thick paste is formed and making sure the butter does not burn.
5 Gradually add the milk, whisking constantly until it is thick and completely smooth.
6 Add the nutmeg and mustard powder, then season with salt and black pepper.
7 Combine the cheeses in a bowl, then add to the sauce gradually while stirring, waiting for each addition of cheese to melt before adding more. Once all the cheese has melted into the sauce, stir in the cream and season to taste.
8 Grease a large ovenproof dish. Pour in the sauce and the pasta, then mix to combine, leaving some extra sauce for the top of the dish.
9 Top with the sauce, breadcrumbs and the extra Parmesan.
10 Bake for 15 minutes or until the top is nice and golden.

Per Serving 317kcals, 26.5g fat (13.3g saturated), 12.5g carbs, 6.5g sugars, 9.2g protein, 1.8g fibre, 0.310g sodium

John Walsh
Winner

DUBLINER

Fartha Riverstick, Co. Cork
"This dish reminds me of my wonderful Aunt Jill, who is my all-time favourite cook. When she makes this dish, I am always by her side measuring and melting the cheese and stirring the macaroni. The time I spend with my Aunt Jill making this dish reminds me of how much I really love cooking."

POTATO CAKES WITH CHEESE AND CHORIZO

Serves 8

5 potatoes, peeled
90g/3oz/⅓ cup butter, plus extra to serve
Salt
60g/2oz/1 cup chorizo (Spanish-style smoked sausage), finely chopped
60g/2oz/½ cup Cheddar, grated
200g/7oz/1½ cups self-raising flour, plus extra for dusting

1 Preheat the oven to 200°C/180°C fan/400°F/gas mark 6. Cover a baking tray with parchment paper.
2 Bring a pot of water to the boil. Add the potatoes and cook for 15 minutes, then drain and mash with two-thirds of the butter and a good pinch of salt.
3 Add the chorizo and Cheddar to the potato mixture.
4 Gradually stir in the flour until the mixture becomes firm.
5 Roll out the dough on a lightly-floured surface into a 2cm/1in thick circle. Cut into eight triangles.
6 Melt the remaining butter in a frying pan over a medium-high heat. When the butter is foaming, add the potato cakes and cook for a few minutes on each side until golden brown and crisp.
7 Transfer to the baking tray and bake in the oven for 10-15 minutes. Serve warm with butter.

Per Serving 256kcals, 7.4g fat (3.9g saturated), 38.9g carbs, 1.6g sugars, 8.3g protein, 3.8g fibre, 0.153g sodium

Alex McLoughlin
Loughrea, Co. Galway
"I call into my Gran on my way home from school and whenever she has leftover potatoes she makes me potato cakes. I now make them myself and I added cheese and chorizo sausage to make them extra tasty. They make a great snack or side dish."

DUBLINER

SIMPLE STEAK SANDWICH

Serves 4

4 x 150g/5oz/0.3lb sirloin or flank steaks
1 tbsp olive oil
6 tbsp mayonnaise, plus extra to spread
3 tbsp wholegrain mustard
1 tbsp honey
4 ciabatta rolls
100g/3.5oz/1 cup Cheddar, grated
Rocket leaves (arugula)
2 tomatoes, sliced
1 red onion, thinly sliced

For the fries:
4 large potatoes
2 tbsp coconut oil
Pinch of smoked papprika
Salt and black pepper

1 Preheat the oven to 200°C/180°C fan/400°F/ gas mark 6. Peel and cut the potatoes into large chips, then place in a glass bowl and cover with boiling water. Microwave on high for five minutes until slightly tender.

2 Remove the potatoes from the water and pat dry with kitchen paper (paper towels).

3 Mix the potatoes with the coconut oil, smoked paprika and some salt and black pepper. Place on a baking tray lined with parchment paper and bake in the oven for 15-20 minutes.

4 Meanwhile, season the steaks with salt and pepper. Heat the oil in a frying pan over a high heat and cook both steaks for 4-5 minutes on one side, then for 3-4 minutes on the other side.

5 Mix the mayonnaise, mustard and honey in a small bowl.

6 Cut the ciabatta rolls in half and sprinkle one side of each with the Cheddar. Place all the rolls in the oven for a few minutes until the cheese melts and the rolls are toasted.

7 Spread the rolls with the mayonnaise mixture and top with the rocket (arugula), tomatoes and red onion. Slice the steak and place on top.

Per Serving 1,143kcals, 43.9g fat (18.7g saturated), 91.8g carbs, 14.8g sugars, 92.9g protein, 12.1g fibre, 0.515g sodium

Clare McCarthy
Shannon, Co. Clare

"Being a mum and the person in the home who does 80% of all the cooking, I am always looking to create tasty, wholesome and quick meals that I can have on the table with little fuss but without any sacrificing flavor. This Simple Steak Sandwich does all that! It is super because everyone in the house loves it so there's no need to cook two or three alternatives. As the cook, seeing clean plates and satisfied faces is what it's all about for me."

DUBLINER

WINTER WARMER SOUP WITH FERMANAGH PUMPKIN BREAD

Serves 4

For the soup:
2 tbsp butter
1 tbsp olive oil
2 carrots, peeled and chopped
2 celery stalks, chopped
1 onion, roughly chopped
120g/4oz/1½ cups red lentils
2 garlic cloves, crushed
500ml/17 fl oz/2 cups vegetable stock
6 tomatoes, chopped
400g/14oz tinned chopped tomatoes, puréed
¼ tsp caraway seeds, toasted
1 small bunch of basil, torn
Salt and black pepper

For the bread:
250g/8oz/2 cups coarse wholemeal flour (wholewheat flour)
60g/2 oz/½ cup plain flour (all-purpose flour)
½ tsp bicarbonate of soda (baking soda)
½ tsp salt
½ tsp oats
60g/2oz/½ cup mixed seeds
30g/1oz/¼ cup chia seeds
300ml/10 fl oz/1½ cups buttermilk
½ tsp butter, melted
½ tsp golden syrup (or honey)

Joyce Dougherty
Donnybrook, Dublin 4

Winner

"Coming from a farming background, this soup and bread are family favourites and conjure up many happy childhood memories. It is a hearty meal, full of goodness, and versatile in that you can easily vary the vegetables depending on the season and what might be available. The caraway seeds offer a background flavour that adds depth, while the crunch of the bread presents another texture and complements the sweetness of the soup. The chia seeds, being a super food, are among the healthiest foods on the planet. On top of that, they (along with the other seeds) make the bread more interesting by enhancing both texture and flavour. The bread is equally delicious toasted with a dollop of butter on top!"

1 Melt the butter and olive oil together in a large saucepan over a low heat.
2 Add the carrots, celery, onion and lentils. Cook for about 10 minutes until soft.
3 Add the garlic and cook for one minute.
4 Add the vegetable stock, stir everything together and bring to the boil.
5 Add all the tomatoes and caraway seeds. Cook for 20 minutes on a low simmer.
6 Remove from the heat and add the basil. Season with salt and pepper to taste. If the soup is too thick, add a little more stock.
7 When the soup is cooked, preheat the oven to 200°C/180°C fan/400°F/gas mark 6 and grease a baking tray.
8 Sieve the flours, bicarbonate of soda (baking soda) and salt into a bowl.
9 Make a well in the centre and add the oats, seeds (reserving some to decorate), buttermilk, melted butter and golden syrup (or honey). Gently mix, then knead together into a dough.
10 Turn the mixture out onto a floured surface, sprinkle the top with the remaining seeds and mark a cross in the top of the dough with a knife.
11 Bake in the oven for 50 minutes.
12 Tip out on a wire tray and leave to cool, then serve with the warm soup.

Per Serving 716kcals, 19.7g fat (5.9g saturated), 110.1g carbs, 20.1g sugars, 26.4g protein, 19.1g fiber, 0.725g sodium

LEMON AND POPPY SEED PANCAKES
Serves 3

2 eggs, lightly beaten
¼ tsp baking powder
3 ripe bananas
2 tsp mixed seeds, plus extra to serve
1 tsp poppy seeds, plus extra to serve
Zest of 1 lemon, plus extra to serve
1 tsp vanilla extract
1 tsp oil

To serve:
3 tsp Greek yoghurt
Maple syrup
Blueberries

1 Mix together the eggs and baking powder in one bowl.
2 Add the bananas to a separate bowl and mash with the back of a fork. Add the seeds, lemon zest and vanilla and mix to combine.
3 Add the egg mixture to the banana mixture, whisking to combine.
4 Heat the oil in a frying pan over a medium heat and cook the pancakes, using two tablespoons of batter for each mini pancake. When bubbles form in the middle of each pancake, flip them over and cook for about one more minute on the other side.
5 Serve with Greek yoghurt, maple syrup, seeds, blueberries and extra lemon zest.

Lili Cronin
Kinsale, Co. Cork
"My super-seed, gluten-free, natural pancakes are delicious and nutritious. They are packed with essential vitamins, minerals, fatty acids and antioxidants. There is no added sugar and these pancakes are delicious at any time of the day. They are the go-to recipe in our house for a healthy breakfast, fast lunch or snack after school."

LINWOODS
YOUR LINK TO GOOD FOOD

Per Serving 215kcals, 17.1g fat (2.8g saturated), 3.1g carbs, 20.1g sugars, 9.7g protein, 2.5g fiber, 0.042g sodium

BLUEBERRY BANANA BREAD

Serves 4

60g/2oz/¼ cup butter, melted, plus extra for greasing
180g/6oz/1 cup light muscavado sugar (or light brown sugar)
120ml/4 fl oz/½ cup buttermilk
1 tsp vanilla extract
1 tsp ground cinnamon
2 medium eggs, lightly beaten
3 ripe bananas, mashed
2 tbsp flaxseed
300g/11oz/2½ cups self-raising flour
1 tsp baking powder
125g/4oz/½ cup frozen blueberries
A handful pumpkin seeds

1 Preheat oven to 180°C/160°C fan/350°F/gas mark 4. Grease 16 mini loaf tins (5x9cm/2x3.5in) with butter, or use one standard 900g/2lb loaf tin.
2 Mix together the butter, sugar, buttermilk, vanilla extract and cinammon in a large bowl.
3 Add the eggs and whisk gently until combined.
4 Stir in the bananas and flaxseed.
5 Sift the flour and baking powder into a separate bowl, then gradually fold this into the banana mixtture until incorporated. Gently fold in the frozen blueberries.
6 Divide the mixture evenly amongst mini loaf tins, or pour into the large loaf tin. Smooth the top with a spatula.
7 Sprinkle over the pumpkin seeds. If using mini loaf tins, arrange them on a baking tray and place in the oven. If using a larger loaf tin, place directly onto the oven rack.
8 Bake for 18-20 minutes (for mini tins) or 45-55 minutes (for a larger tin), until a skewer inserted into the centre comes out clean. The centre of the loaf should be firm to touch when fully baked. Leave inside the tins for five minutes before turning out onto a wire rack to cool completely before serving.

Per Serving 509kcals, 13.8g fat (7.5g saturated), 84.8g carbs, 15.9g sugars, 12.9g protein, 5.4g fiber, 0.139g sodium

Lisa Naylor
Dublin

"Last year I entered a residential facility for treatment of depression and the eating disorder I had been battling for eight years. Six weeks later, I baked my first banana bread, using my own recipe. Back at home I continued baking for others and, eventually, the day came when I was able to taste my handiwork: the banana bread. The past year has been difficult, but regaining my love of baking has given me hope that I can take back everything else I have lost. This recipe represents my ongoing journey to recovery, and how far I've already come."

MINI CHICKEN PAPRIKA POTS

Serves 4

1 tbsp vegetable oil
30g/1oz/2 tbsp butter
½ a small leek, thinly sliced
1 garlic clove, crushed
200g/7oz/4 cups mushrooms, sliced
2 tsp smoked paprika
30g/1oz/¼ cup plain flour (all-purpose flour)
120ml/4oz/½ cup chicken stock
300ml/11 fl oz/1¼ cups milk
Salt and black pepper
2 red peppers, roughly chopped
250g/8oz/0.5lb cooked chicken, shredded
60g/2oz/½ cup breadcrumbs
1 tsp fresh parsley, chopped
30g/1oz/¼ cup Cheddar, grated

To serve:
Baby tomatoes
Cucumbers, sliced into chunks
Baby potatoes, baked

1 Preheat the oven to 200°C/180°C fan/400°F/gas mark 6 and lightly grease four ramekins.
2 Heat the oil and butter in a large saucepan over a medium-high heat. Add the leek and garlic and sauté for two minutes. Add mushrooms and cook for further 2-3 minutes.
3 Stir in the paprika and flour to coat.
4 Add the stock and milk and season with salt and pepper. Bring to the boil, then reduce the heat and simmer, stirring frequently, until thickened.
5 Stir in the peppers and chicken. Simmer for five minutes, then divide the mixture evenly between the ramekins.
6 Mix together the breadcrumbs, parsley and grated Cheddar with salt and pepper, then sprinkle over the ramekins. Bake in the oven for 15 minutes until crispy and golden on top.
7 Meanwhile, thread the tomatoes and cucumber pieces onto skewers. Serve the ramekins hot with baked potatoes and the skewered vegetables.

Per Serving 349kcals, 14.8g fat (6.6g saturated), 26.6g carbs, 7.2g sugars, 27.8g protein, 2.3g fiber, 0.38g sodium

Holly Meehan
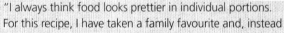
Gorey, Co. Wexford

"I always think food looks prettier in individual portions. For this recipe, I have taken a family favourite and, instead of serving on a bed of rice, I have potted it and topped it with breadcrumbs and cheese, making little pies. Of course you could do the same in one big casserole! The sauce is quick and easy to make. This makes for a fast, tasty and nutritious meal even when time is tight. The choice of smoked paprika was by chance really – one day I used smoked paprika by mistake, but my family found it tastier than the plain paprika, so now we always use it."

CHICKEN AND SWEET POTATO FRITTATA

Serves 2-4

6 eggs
100ml/3.5 fl oz/½ cup milk
2 tbsp fresh parsley, finely chopped
Salt and black pepper
140g/5oz/0.3lb cooked chicken, shredded
1 medium sweet potato, peeled and grated
1 red onion, finely chopped

To serve:
3 garlic cloves, crushed
60g/2oz/¼ cup butter, softened
1 baguette, halved

1 Preheat oven to 200°C/180°C fan/400°F/gas mark 6 and coat a 20cm/8in round baking dish with cooking spray.
2 Beat the eggs in a jug and whisk in the milk, parsley, salt and pepper.
3 Mix in the chicken, grated sweet potato and onion. Pour into the baking dish and bake in the oven for 30 minutes.
4 Meanwhile, mix the garlic with the butter and spread onto the inside of the bread. Wrap the bread in foil and bake for 15-20 minutes. Serve the frittata warm with the garlic bread.

Per Serving 295cals, 18.6g fat (8.8g saturated), 11.1g carbs, 4.7g sugars, 21.6g protein, 1.7g fibre, 0.230g sodium

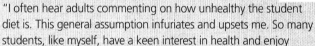

Amy Meegan
Castleblayney, Co. Monaghan
"I often hear adults commenting on how unhealthy the student diet is. This general assumption infuriates and upsets me. So many students, like myself, have a keen interest in health and enjoy cooking nutritious meals. This recipe means a lot to be because it is something quick and easy that I can whip up and pop in the oven when I get in from a long day of lectures. As well as being hassle-free, it is delicious with a healthy balance of protein, slow-release carbohydrates and vegetables."

Greene FARM

CHICKEN SUPREME BAKE
Serves 4

2 tbsp olive oil
1 onion, finely chopped
150g/5oz/3 cups mushrooms, finely chopped
1 red pepper, chopped
2cm/1in piece of root ginger, grated
400g/14oz/1¾ cups condensed mushroom soup
125ml/4 fl oz/½ cup water
200g/7oz/0.5lb cooked chicken, shredded
Salt and black pepper
2 tbsp parsley, chopped
60g/2oz/½ cup breadcrumbs
30g/1oz/¼ cup Cheddar, grated

1 Preheat the oven to 200°C/180°C fan/400°F/gas mark 6. Heat the olive oil in a frying pan over a medium-high heat and add the onion, mushrooms and red pepper. Cook for three minutes until soft.
2 Stir in the ginger and cook for 30 seconds. Stir in the soup and water, cover with a lid and simmer for five minutes.
3 Add the chicken and warm through. Season well and add the parsley.
4 Divide the chicken mixture between four ramekins, then top with the breadcrumbs and Cheddar. Bake in the oven for 25 minutes or until golden brown on top.

Per Serving 714kcals, 42.1g fat (11.1g saturated), 66.5g carbs, 16.2g sugars, 22.8g protein, 9.3g fibre, 0.651g sodium

Julie Newport
Kilbritain, Co. Cork
"This recipe is very important to me because my mother has been making this for me ever since I was a young girl. I enjoy it so much and I hope you enjoy it too. It's an easy and tasty meal; there will definitely be nothing left on the plate!"

LUNCHBOX MUFFINS

Serves 6

1 tsp oil
½ red onion, finely chopped
½ red pepper, finely chopped
3 slices of ham, finely chopped
100g/3.5oz/1 cup mature Cheddar,
grated
4 eggs, lightly beaten
1 tsp olive oil
125ml/4 fl oz/½ cup milk
½ tsp baking powder
Salt and black pepper

1 Preheat the oven to 200°C/180°C
  fan/400°F/gas mark 6 and coat a 6-cup
  muffin tin with cooking spray. Heat the
  oil in a frying pan over a medium heat
  and cook the onion, pepper and ham
  for two minutes until softened.
2 Fill the muffin cups with the ham and
  vegetable mixture. Top each with some
  of the grated cheese.
3 Mix the eggs, oil, milk, baking powder,
  salt and pepper in a jug.
4 Pour the egg mixture into each of the
  muffin cups until they are almost full.
5 Bake the muffins in the oven for 20
  minutes until they are golden brown.
6 Allow to cool for about five minutes
  before removing from the tin.

Per Serving 69kcals, 3.5g fat (1.0g saturated), 4.5g carbs, 1.6g
sugars, 5.1g protein, 1.2g fiber, 0.367g sodium

Grace Quigley
Carrickmines, Dublin 18   Winner   easy parenting

"I love this recipe because I can make it all by myself. It uses simple
and cheap ingredients that I chose because I think they would appeal
to children my age. It is also easy to make. It is a very tasty school lunch and makes a
nice break from eating sandwiches every day! My teacher is happy too because we have
a Healthy Lunch Rule in school, and this lunch is very healthy. I like that my Dad and little
brother love eating these too!"

PIZZA WHEELS
Makes 6

200g/7oz/1½ cups plain flour (all-purpose flour)
100g/3.5oz/½ cup cold butter, cubed
3 tbsp cold water, plus extra if needed
80g/3oz/⅓ cup tomato purée (tomato paste)
8 slices of pepperoni, chopped
75g/2.5oz/⅔ cup Mozzarella, grated
75g/2.5oz/⅔ cup Cheddar, grated

1 Preheat the oven to 200°C/180°C fan/400°F/gas mark 6 and line a baking tray with parchment paper. Sieve the flour into a bowl. Rub in butter with your fingers until the mixture resembles breadcrumbs.
2 Add the water and mix until a dough is formed, adding more water if necessary.
3 Knead the dough on a floured surface and roll into a rectangle. Spread the tomato purée (tomato paste) into an even layer, then sprinkle over the pepperoni and cheeses.
4 Roll up the pastry like a swiss roll, starting from one of the long ends. Cut into even slices, place onto the baking tray and bake for 15-20 minutes.

Alía Naughton
Ballygar, Co. Galway

easy parenting

"I have twin brothers, Michael and Anthony, and as you can imagine there are a lot of hungry boys to feed. I have made the pizza wheels many times varying the ingredients. I often use pineapple, corn, mushrooms and tomato, but the pizza wheels that have been a favourite in our house are pepperoni and cheese. They are very tasty, and because they are small it is easy for children to carry them around and eat them on the go."

Per Serving 547kcals, 36.1g fat (12.3g saturated), 38.9g carbs, 0.9g sugars, 16.3g protein, 1.4g fiber, 0.120g sodium

GLUTEN- AND DAIRY-FREE FLAPJACKS

Serves 10

125g/4oz/½ cup dairy-free margarine
60ml/2 fl oz/3 tbsp golden syrup (or honey)
60g/2oz/⅓ cup brown sugar
200g/7oz/1¼ cups pure oats (gluten-free oats)
3 tbsp sesame seeds

Let your kids help you choose any two; use a handful of each:
Mixed fruit
Dried cranberries
Raisins
Chocolate chips (dairy-free)
Sultanas
Dried apricots, chopped

1 Preheat the oven to 200°C/180°C fan/400°F/gas mark 6 and line a large baking dish with parchment paper.

2 Melt the margarine, golden syrup (or honey) and brown sugar in a saucepan over a medium heat.

3 Mix the oats, sesame seeds and any mix-in choices in a large bowl. Pour the melted syrup mixture into the bowl and mix well.

4 Use a spatula to spread the mixture into the baking dish in an even layer.

5 Bake for 20-25 minutes until golden brown. Leave to cool slightly before slicing into squares.

Per Serving 154kcals, 2.6g fat (0.0g saturated), 30.7g carbs, 11.3g sugars, 3.2g protein, 2.7g fiber, 0.142g sodium

Laura Kenny
Gorey, Co. Wexford

"Flapjacks are a healthy and filling treat. They are handy for lunchboxes, as after-school snacks or for popping into the picnic bag for a day out. The kids love helping with these; they decide what combination of fruit or chocolate chips to put in them, so get them involved and have fun! My kids have food allergies and I love this recipe as it is free from many of the main food allergens, so is already suitable for them or can be easily adapted as required."

easy parenting

CHICKEN FAJITAS WITH GUACAMOLE AND SALSA

Serves 4

For the fajitas:
2 peppers (1 red and 1 yellow), deseeded and sliced
1 onion, thinly sliced
2 chicken fillets, sliced into long strips
A pinch of ground cumin
1 tsp paprika
Juice of 1 lime
1 tbsp olive oil, plus extra for cooking
Black pepper

For the salsa:
12 cherry tomatoes, roughly chopped
½ red chilli, deseeded and finely chopped
1 small bunch of fresh coriander (cilantro), chopped
Juice of 1 lime
1 tbsp olive oil
Salt and black pepper

For the guacamole:
2 ripe avocados
8 cherry tomatoes, roughly chopped
1 red chilli, deseeded and finely chopped
1 tbsp fresh coriander (cilantro), chopped
Juice of 1 lime

To serve:
6 small flour tortillas
75g/2.5oz/⅔ cup Cheddar, grated
150ml/5 fl oz/⅔ cup natural (plain) yoghurt

1 Combine all of the ingredients for the fajitas in a resealable plastic bag and mix until thoroughly coated.
2 Combine all of the ingredients for the salsa in a small bowl.
3 Halve and stone the avocados, then chop the flesh. Add to a separate bowl, then mix in the rest of the ingredients for the guacamole.
4 Heat some oil in a pan over a medium-high heat and cook the fajita mixture, stirring, for 6-8 minutes until the chicken is cooked through.
5 Warm the tortillas in a microwave or a warm oven until soft and pliable.
6 Serve the chicken fajita mix in the warm tortillas with bowls of the Cheddar, yoghurt, guacamole and salsa. Fill the wraps to your liking and serve immediately.

Per Serving 770kcals, 35g fat (8.4g saturated), 46.3g carbs, 24.3g sugars, 76.3g protein, 16.7g fiber, 0.154g sodium

Winner

Chelsea Sutherland Moy park
Cloyne, Co. Cork
"I cooked this dish for my Home Economics cookery practical as part of my transition year summer exams. I thought it was simple to prepare and also tastes delicious. It soon became a Friday night favourite with my family and a fun dish to make for a girls' night in with friends."

JUMPIN' JAMBALYA

Serves 4-6

3 tbsp olive oil
185g/6oz/1 cup rice
1 onion, finely chopped
2 garlic cloves, crushed
1 red pepper, chopped
2 tomatoes, chopped
150g/5oz/2½ cups spicy chorizo
(Spanish-style smoked sausage),
chopped
2 large chicken fillets, chopped into
bite-sized pieces
1 pinch of saffron threads
¼ tsp cayenne pepper
¼ tsp tumeric
1 tsp of paprika
½ tsp Cajun seasoning
500ml/17 fl oz/2 cups chicken stock
Salt and black pepper
1 lemon, cut into wedges

1 Heat the oil in a large, deep frying
   pan over a medium heat, add the
   uncooked rice and fry for one minute.
   Add the onion, garlic, pepper,
   tomatoes, chorizo and the chicken. Fry
   the mixture, stirring, for five minutes.
2 Add the saffron, cayenne pepper,
   tumeric, paprika and Cajun seasoning.
   Stir to coat.
3 Stir in the chicken stock. Reduce the
   heat, cover with a lid and simmer for
   20-25 minutes, stirring a few times
   throughout, until all the stock has been
   absorbed. Season with salt and pepper.
4 Squeeze over a bit of lemon juice and
   serve hot.

Per Serving 406kcals, 20.8g fat (5.7g saturated), 30.5g carbs,
3g sugars, 23.4g protein, 1.9g fibre, 0.629g sodium

Anna-Jane Kingston
Salthill, Co. Galway
"This flavourful fusion dish reminds me of my colourful friends
and family. It's bright, cheerful and hopping with taste – great
for entertaining a crowd. I describe this recipe as one of my one-pot wonders as it's
delightfully easy to prepare, you can jazz it up in different ways each time you make
it and there's never a morsel left at the end. All in all, it's bursting with flavour and
character and helps create a wonderfully happy eating environment."

Moy
park

PARMESAN CHICKEN GOUJONS

Serves 4

450g/16oz/1lb chicken fillets, sliced
30g/1oz/¼ cup plain flour (all-purpose flour)
Salt and black pepper
2 eggs, lightly beaten
60g/2oz/½ cup breadcrumbs
60g/2oz/½ cup Parmesan, finely grated
2 tbsp vegetable oil

For the dipping sauce:
2 tbsp sweet chilli sauce
4 tbsp mayonnaise

For the salad:
Mixed leaves
Strawberries, sliced
1 kiwi, peeled and sliced
Red and green seedless grapes
Blueberries

1 Preheat the oven to 200°C/180°C fan/400°F/gas mark 6. Coat a baking tray with cooking spray and place in the oven to warm.
2 Mix the flour with some salt and pepper in a shallow bowl. Place the beaten eggs in a second bowl, and the breadcrumbs and grated Parmesan in a third.
3 Remove the tray from the oven. Coat the chicken strips in the flour, shaking off any excess. Dip in the eggs, then coat in the Parmesan breadcrumbs.
4 Arrange the chicken in a single layer on the tray. Return to the oven and bake for 12-18 minutes, turning over halfway through, until golden brown and cooked through.
5 Toss the mixed leaves with the strawberries, kiwi, grapes and blueberries.
6 Mix the sweet chilli sauce and mayonnaise in a small bowl. Serve with the hot goujons and the fruity salad.

Per Serving 547kcals, 36.1g fat (12.3g saturated), 38.9g carbs, 0.9g sugars, 16.3g protein, 1.4g fiber, 0.120g sodium

Kelly Coghlan
Garrettstown, Co. Cork

Moy park

"I chose to make Parmesan chicken goujons because they are a nutritious, delicious, quick meal. I love being able to make my own goujons as you know what goes into them and it's a simple recipe. Also, I decided to serve mixed leaves with fruit because I love the sweet flavours of the fruit with the refreshing salad. This salad is very healthy with plenty of vitamins in the fruit and lots of green in the mixed leaves. The sweet chilli mayonnaise is a gorgeous contrast with the crunchy tender chicken goujons."

LEMON POLENTA CAKE

Serves 8-10

For the cake:
175g/6oz/¾ cup butter, softened, plus extra for greasing
200g/7oz/1 cup caster sugar (superfine sugar)
3 eggs, lightly beaten
75g/2.5oz/½ cup polenta
200g/7oz/2 cups ground almonds
1 tsp gluten-free baking powder
Zest and juice of 2 lemons

For the candied lemons:
250ml/8 fl oz/1 cup water
175g/6oz/¾ cup caster sugar (superfine sugar)
Zest of 1 large lemon

1 Preheat the oven to 160°C/140°C fan/325°F/gas mark 3. Grease a 23cm/9in round springform tin and line the base with parchment paper.

2 With an electric mixer, cream the butter and 175g/6oz/¾ cup of the sugar until fluffy. Gradually beat in the eggs one at a time.

3 Add the polenta, almonds, baking powder and lemon zest and mix thoroughly.

4 Scrape the mixture into the prepared tin and smooth the surface.

5 Bake for 50-60 minutes until springy to the touch (it will not rise much). Leave to cool slightly in the tin.

6 Meanwhile, stir the lemon juice and the remaining sugar in a small saucepan over a medium heat. Remove from the heat when dissolved.

7 While the cake is still warm, turn it out onto a wire rack. Remove the parchment paper, then flip the cake back over on the rack. Poke holes into the top of the cake with a toothpick, then slowly pour the hot lemon syrup evenly over the surface.

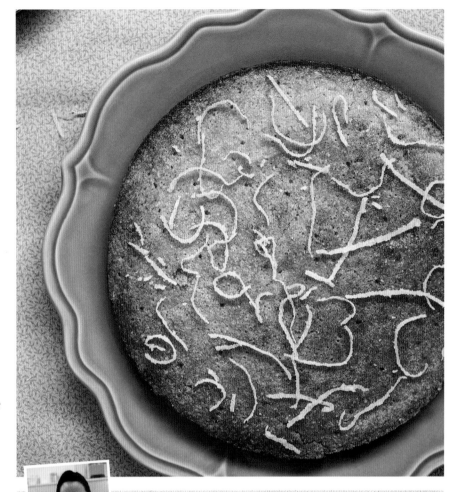

Ann-Marie Lavery
Bray, Co. Wicklow

"Wherever I bring this cake, it is always the first to disappear and I spend the night taking everyone's email addresses to send on the recipe! It's such a crowd pleaser, especially for any coeliacs as they can relax and enjoy it. I bill the cake as being wheat-free and gluten-free, but not taste-free!"

8 For the candied lemons, bring the water and half of the sugar to boil in a saucepan. When the sugar dissolves, reduce to a simmer and add the lemon zest.

9 Simmer for about 20 minutes or until the lemon pieces are translucent.

10 Heat the oven to 120°C/100°C fan/250°F/gas mark ¼. Drain the lemon pieces and transfer to a baking tray lined with parchment paper.

11 Sprinkle the rest of the sugar over the lemon zest, then bake for 20 minutes or until they have begun to harden.

12 Decorate the cake with the candied lemons to serve.

Per Serving 363kcals, 25.6g fat (10.2g saturated), 30.6g carbs, 21.1g sugars, 6.6g protein, 2.7g fibre, 0.120g sodium

BROWNIE PIZZA SLICE
Serves 8

100g/3.5oz/⅓ cup dark chocolate
100g/3.5oz/½ cup butter
200g/7oz/1 cup brown sugar
3 large eggs, lightly beaten
200g/7oz/1½ cups self-raising flour
2 tbsp cocoa powder
150g/5oz/½ cup Rolo chocolates,
roughly chopped
120g/4oz/⅓ cup Maltesers (chocolate-
covered malt balls), roughly chopped
4 tbsp caramel sauce

1 Preheat the oven 200°C/180°C fan/400°F/
   gas mark 6. Grease and line a 23cm/9in
   round baking tin with parchment paper.
2 Melt the chocolate and butter in a
   saucepan over a low heat. Turn off the
   heat and gradually stir in the sugar and
   the eggs.
3 Sift in the flour and cocoa powder and stir
   to combine.
4 Spread into the tin. Sprinkle over most of
   the chopped Rolos and Maltesers, then
   press down into the batter.
5 Bake for 20 minutes until the edges are
   set but the middle is still slightly soft.
   Remove from the oven and top with the
   remaining chocolates.
6 Drizzle with the caramel sauce and slice
   into wedges to serve.

Amy Ryan
Navan, Co. Meath
"I absolutely love baking for my family and this recipe is a huge hit!
It's my Mum's recipe but I have given it my own twist. Who can
say no to a slice of brownie pizza – a squidgy brownie topped with
Rolos and Maltesers. Being vision impaired, taste is very important to me and this very
easy recipe is just brownie heaven."

Connacht Gold

Per Serving 554kcals, 24.1g fat (12.0g saturated), 78.2g carbs,
42.4g sugars, 8.2g protein, 1.6g fibre, 0.191g sodium

ZUCCHINI LASAGNE

Serves 8

2 tbsp olive oil
1 garlic clove, crushed
1kg/35oz/2.2lb courgette (zucchini), thinly sliced
Salt and black pepper
1 tsp chives, finely chopped
1 tsp basil leaves, coarsely chopped
80g/3oz/⅓ cup butter
80g/3oz/⅔ cup plain flour (all-purpose flour)
700ml/23 fl oz/3 cups milk, warmed
A pinch of nutmeg
2 balls of fresh buffalo Mozzerella, sliced into cubes
60g/2oz/⅔ cup Parmesan, grated, plus extra for topping
80g/3oz/½ cup pine nuts
12 courgette (zucchini) flowers, cleaned
250g/8oz/½ lb fresh lasagne sheets

1. Preheat the oven to 180°C/160°C fan/350°F/gas mark 4 and coat a baking dish with cooking spray.
2. Heat the oil in a large frying pan over a medium heat and cook the garlic and courgette (zucchini) for 3-5 minutes.
3. Season with salt and pepper, then add the chives and basil. Turn off the heat and set aside.
4. Melt the butter in a saucepan over a medium heat. Whisk in the flour until a paste forms.
5. Gradually whisk in the milk, whisking constantly to avoid lumps. Keep stirring until the sauce thickens, and as soon as the first bubbles begin to appear, cook for 4-5 minutes.
6. Add some salt, black pepper and the nutmeg. Remove from the heat and set aside.
7. In a bowl, mix the cooked courgette mixture, Mozzerella, Parmesan and pine nuts. Season with salt and pepper.
8. Gently tear the flowers by hand and stir them into the courgette mixture.
9. Spread one-third of the white sauce into the bottom of the baking dish, then add half of the lasagne sheets, trimming to fit if needed.
10. Add half of the courgette mixture, spreading into an even layer. Repeat these layers, ending with the white sauce on top.
11. Sprinkle over some Parmesan and bake for 35 minutes until bubbling. Serve hot.

Per Serving 455kcals, 28.6g fat (11.9g saturated), 32.4g carbs, 6.9g sugars, 20.9g protein, 2g fibre, 0.372g sodium

Elisabetta Ravarino
Celbridge, Co. Kildare

"This dish reminds me of long summer evenings in Italy with all of my family gathered at the dinner table under the big magnolia tree in the garden. I was brought up in the north of Italy with my grandfather and parents, and we grew our own vegetables and fruit. My mother spent a large part of each day cooking with our own produce. Every enthusiastic vegetable grower (and I am one) knows how easy and proliferous zucchini are. This dish is a change from the more traditional red Bolognese lasagne; it's delicious and a guaranteed winner with all my guests, vegetarian or not."

Kitchen basics

HOW TO COOL FOOD SAFELY

DO make sure that food is cooled quickly. Take food out of the larger container it was cooked in and carefully put it into smaller, shallow containers so it will cool faster; large pieces of meat can be divided into smaller portions for the same reason.

Why? The longer food takes to cool, the more time bacteria have to multiply, potentially causing food poisoning.

DON'T leave cooked food out for more than two hours.

Why? Unless refrigerated, illness-causing bacteria can grow in perishable foods.

DO put the cooled food into the fridge or freezer after a maximum two-hour period.

Why? Once food has cooled to room temperature, it should be brought down to below 5°C/40°F within the next four hours to prevent bacterial growth.

DON'T put hot food straight into the fridge.

Why? It may cause the internal fridge temperature to rise for a short time, putting all other food stored in the fridge at risk of being in the temperature "danger zone" for too long.

HOW TO PROPERLY DEFROST YOUR FREEZER

1 Turn off the freezer.

2 Empty all the food and place it in plastic bags.

3 Place old newspapers and towels at the base of the freezer to soak up the water as it melts.

4 Wipe the inside of the freezer with a hot cloth.

5 Remove and wash any removable parts, such as ice trays and drawers.

6 Place a bowl of hot water in the freezer until the ice has melted.

7 Once melted, dry the freezer and clean it with an anti-bacterial cleaning solution.

• For even faster thawing, prop a fan on a chair. Turn it on and let it blow into the freezer for about one hour.

• You can use a blow drier to speed up the melting process for larger chunks of ice. Be extra careful that no wires come into contact with water.

• To slow ice build-up, wipe the inside of the freezer with kitchen paper (paper towel) coated in vegetable oil.

TO KEEP OR NOT TO KEEP?

Read on and learn how long you can safely store foods in your cupboard, fridge and freezer

CUPBOARD		FRIDGE		FREEZER	
BREAD	5–7 DAYS	POULTRY	1–2 DAYS	DELI MEAT	1–2 MONTHS
PEANUT BUTTER	6 MONTHS	FRUIT	2 DAYS	FISH	2–6 MONTHS
CEREAL	1 YEAR	BREAD DOUGH AND PASTRY	3–4 DAYS	MINCE	3–4 MONTHS
RICE	1 YEAR			STEAKS	6–12 MONTHS
TINNED GOODS	1 YEAR	STEAK	3–5 DAYS	POULTRY	1 YEAR
SALAD DRESSING	1 YEAR	LEFTOVERS	4 DAYS	BREAD	1 YEAR
JAM AND SYRUP	1 YEAR	CHEESE	1–2 WEEKS	FRESH VEGGIES	1 YEAR
PASTA	2 YEARS	EGGS	3–5 WEEKS	FRESH FRUIT	1 YEAR
		BUTTER	3 MONTHS		

10 DEADLY KITCHEN SINS
ARE YOU GUILTY OF ANY OF THE BELOW?

1 Overcrowding the pan.
When you're in a hurry, it's tempting to pile too much food into a pan or onto a baking tray. However, a packed pan generates steam, making food limp and preventing food from browning properly.

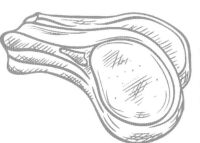

2 Not letting meat rest. Eating meat as soon as it's cooked means it'll never be as tender as it should be. All meat, even chicken fillets, benefits from a few minutes resting on a warm plate, covered loosely with foil. This allows it to relax and retain its juices, making your dinner tastier and more succulent. A good rule of thumb is to allow one minute of resting time for every 100g/¼lb of meat.

3 Cooking meat straight from the fridge. If you put a cold piece of meat straight into a hot pan or oven, you risk drying out the exterior before the inside has a chance to cook through. If you want your meat to cook evenly, let it come to room temperature first.

4 Not being prepared.
A wise cook reads the recipe through at least once before it's time to get started. There's nothing worse than realising you were supposed to marinate the meat overnight, or that you've forgotten a vital ingredient. Get into the chef's habit of mise en place: having all of the ingredients prepped before you get cooking.

5 Turning food too often.
Over-enthusiastic turning, prodding and poking of the food in a pan will mean it takes longer to cook. It'll also result in drier meat, as the more it's moved, the more liquid it will release. Be patient and give it time to cook on one side before turning over.

6 Not giving the pan enough time to get hot.
If the oil isn't hot enough, your food will stick to the pan. Always heat an empty pan for at least 1-2 minutes; the pan is ready when you can hold your hand three inches above it and feel the heat radiating. Now add the fat, waiting for oil to shimmer and butter to foam before beginning to cook.

7 Boiling when you should simmer. When liquid is at a simmer, a bubble will break the surface every second or two. If it's bubbling more vigorously than that, the liquid is at a boil. The difference can have a big impact to cooked food.

8 Being impatient with caramelised onions.
Caramelising is not the same as sautéing. It takes at least 20 minutes, and if the heat is too high, the onions will burn, so keep it at medium-low. Don't take them off too early, either; they should be a rich brown, much-reduced, and soft but not mushy.

9 Forgetting to taste as you go.
Recipes don't always call for the "right" amount of seasoning, cooking times may be estimates, and results vary depending on ingredients, your oven and countless other factors. You need to taste as you go to remain in control.

10 Boiling pasta in a small pot. When you add pasta to a small amount of water, it lowers the temperature substantially more than if you put it in lots of water, so the water will take longer to return to a boil. In the meantime, the pasta sits at the bottom of the pot, sticking together and becoming mushy.

Nutritional information key

- € Budget-Friendly
- ❄ Freezable
- ☺ Kid-Friendly
- ✕ Dairy-Free
- V Vegetarian
- LF Low-Fat
- DF Diabetes-Friendly
- GF Gluten-Free